THE GREAT AMERICAN WEB BOOK

THE GREAT AMERICAN WEB BOOK

A Citizen's Guide to the Treasures of the U.S. Government on the World Wide Web

RAPHAEL SAGALYN

and the

Staff of *Inside Information*

TIMES BUSINESS

RANDOM HOUSE

Staff
The Great American Web Book

Managing Editor
Chris Grams

Random House Editor
Jon Karp

Chief Researchers
Erika Grams
Raphael Sagalyn

Researchers
Lisa Adams
Nicolas Audy-Rowland
Jenny Bent
Ethan Kline
Howard Means
Kristen Wainwright

Sagalyn, Raphael.
    The great American Web book : a citizen's guide to the treasures
of the U.S. government on the World Wide Web / Raphael Sagalyn and
the staff of Inside information.
        p.   cm.
    Includes index.
    ISBN 0-8129-2814-8 (alk. paper)
    1. World Wide Web (Information retrieval system)—Directories.
2. Government information—United States—Computer network
resources—Directories.   I. Inside information (Washington, D.C.)
II. Title.
ZA4226.S24   1996
025.04—dc20   96-25785

Random House website address: http://www.randomhouse.com/

Printed in the United States of America on acid-free paper.

9 8 7 6 5 4 3 2

First Edition

*To Mother and Dad, my love and gratitude
for always being my Net.*

*And to Anne, Rebecca, and Erica
for the good fortune of our wonderful family.*

Acknowledgments

Toward the end of the few months when I was immersed in research for this book, my daughters issued this sobering refrain: "Are you done with your book yet Dad?" Yes, girls, at least until the revised edition. My wife, Anne, and Rebecca and Erica were completely understanding of my longer hours at the office, my Saturday afternoons and Sunday mornings away from home, the ringing static of modem connections at five in the morning. Anne gave up a lot of Saturdays in the fields with Penny; I'm grateful for that and for your newfound interest in electronic life. And girls, when you write your books, we'll have this small book to mark these heady, early days of the Net. My love to all three of you, and to Remy, too.

Thanks to my colleagues at my packaging firm, Inside Information, who have all been so supportive of this book. A special note of thanks to: Erika Grams, who unearthed the first wows!; Chris Grams, the Webmaster; Richard Heller, advisor and friend; and to Nancy Marcus Land and her colleagues at Publications Development Company of Texas, for their thorough effort in emending and designing the text.

Thanks especially to Jon Karp of Random House and Peter Osnos of Times Books for giving me the chance. Thanks to friends Graeme Bush and Jim Graham for business counsel and those great dinners (one of you is next); to Mark and Brian for I don't know what, to Matthew for what once was, to my sister Ann and my brother Jim, for always being there for me, and most of all to my parents, for everything.

Contents

x   Contents

Independent Establishments and Quasi-Official Agencies   115

A Guide to the Sidebars

Introduction

So what has your government done for you lately? It is altogether fitting and proper to ask this question.

The answer is: A lot more than you think. Amid all the hoopla and genuine excitement over the Internet, Uncle Sam's contributions stand out and there are three reasons why we've devoted a book to your government's presence on the World Wide Web.

Reason 1. The U.S. government is arguably home to the most frequently visited and most highly praised websites in the universe. The Library of Congress, for example, fields more than one million "hits" (or visits) each day, according to its Librarian, James H. Billington. The White House, NASA, and the CIA are also among the most popular sites on the World Wide Web. In its year-end issue of 1995, *Business Week* cited the "six hottest sites," three of which are in Uncle Sam's domain—at the Census Bureau, the Federal Reserve, and the Securities and Exchange Commission.

Reason 2. The government has a simple and special connection to the Internet: it basically invented it.

A little history is in order. In 1964, the RAND Corporation, the famous think tank for military strategy, asked a simple question: How would political and military leaders communicate with one another in the event of a nuclear war? A RAND proposal recognized the need for a communications network that would have no central authority (an absence that would make the network "safe"); information would be routed from node to node. Five years later, in 1969, the first nodes were installed at UCLA and the fledgling system was named ARPAnet, because it was largely funded by the Advanced Research Projects Agency at the

Department of Defense. Scientists, researchers, and government officials could then transfer data along high-speed transmission lines.

In 1973, the Defense Department began to connect ARPAnet to other local networks around the country, creating a system of interconnected networks that would still function in the event of a military attack. This linking was called the "Internetting project."

In 1982, ARPAnet switched to a new, more efficient communications "protocol" (the language that computers speak to one another) that allowed the linking of ARPAnet to other local networks, at other government agencies and at universities. And in 1986, the National Science Foundation put into place a communications infrastructure called NSFnet, which linked supercomputers through regional networks at other government agencies such as the Department of Energy and the National Institutes of Health.

Finally, in 1989, ARPAnet expired, its mission accomplished and what soon arose in its stead was what we call the Internet and the acceptance of the basic Internet "domains of the World Wide Web," which refer to those three-letter units that end almost every website, such as "gov," "mil," "edu," "com," "org," and "net."

There you have it; an all too brief history of an extraordinary future. For this background, I'd like to acknowledge Bruce Sterling's excellent history of the Internet (http://w3.aces.uiuc.edu/aim/scale/nethistory .html) as well as a fine series of publications issued by the Library of Congress, called "Brief Guides to the Internet," accessible at (http:// lcweb.loc.gov/loc/guides). The individual titles include:

Overview of the Internet

Internet Glossary

Connecting to the Internet

Internet Addresses

Internet Navigation Tools

Locating Information on the Internet

Saving Information from the Internet

Government Information on the Internet

Library of Congress Internet Resources

Using the Internet to Communicate with Others

Setting Up a Web Server

Reason 3. Uncle Sam is the single largest source of information in the world, and the rise of the World Wide Web has made the government's information riches accessible to anyone with a computer and a modem.

Researchers in any field of endeavor will find authoritative data from agencies like the Commerce and Labor Departments and the Public Health Service (which encompasses the National Institutes of Health). Teachers will find the country's largest source of educational information at ERIC, the Educational Research Information Center, and its sixteen clearinghouses, all sponsored by the Education Department. Scientists can explore the findings of their peers at hundreds of locations inside the government, such as Los Alamos, Oak Ridge and the other national laboratories affiliated with the Energy Department.

But you don't need to be a specialist to appreciate the treasures of Uncle Sam's presence on the World Wide Web. Here's a sampling of what you can do with a simple click of the mouse:

► Click on the U.S. Postal Service and get the most current rates of any class of postage and any zip code.

► Click on The JASON Project at NASA and participate in global explorations of the ocean, using advanced interactive telecommunications.

► Click on Civil War Battlefields at the Interior Department and get an index of battlefield sites, casualty figures, commanders, and more.

► Click on the U.S. House of Representatives, find your Congressperson's e-mail, and let your "voice" be heard.

► Click on the U.S. Geological Survey and download maps and actual lesson plans for teaching geography.

▶ Visit the Charters of Freedom—photos and complete text of the Declaration of Independence and the Constitution, with accompanying articles on their history—at the National Archives.

▶ Consult the card catalog of the Library of Congress or the encyclopedic World Factbook at the CIA.

▶ Get the most up-to-date information on almost any ailment or disease at the Centers for Disease Control and the National Institutes of Health.

▶ Print hard-to-find forms from the IRS.

▶ Send an e-mail letter to the President, using an online form at the White House.

You'll also find other wonderful interactive tools such as these:

▶ Enter the name of any town or city in the National Weather Service and you'll get a short- or long-term forecast (even ski conditions) from the most reliable of all weather sources.

▶ Enter the name of any town or city in the U.S. Gazetteer at the Commerce Department and you'll get a population report and other crucial demographic indicators.

▶ Enter the name of any public company into the EDGAR database at the Securities and Exchange Commission and get critical investment information.

▶ Or, just for fun, type in your first or last name and ask the Name Frequency Database to determine where your names rank in popularity according to the 1990 Census.

I could go on to underscore the usefulness of the information now online from Uncle Sam, but I would be overlooking some of the Internet's greatest pleasures. Think about NASA for a moment. Imagine being able to see the latest color photos from the Hubble Telescope or Mars Explorer or watching the landing of the Space Shuttle on NASA-TV, or having a front-row seat at a virtual movie-and-slide show of the history of space exploration. Think about the Smithsonian; even better, visit all eleven museums, from the Air and Space Museum to the Freer Gallery to the National Museum of American History, where floors of exhibits are available for your viewing pleasure with the simple click of the mouse.

In *The Great American Web Book,* my staff of researchers and I have traveled deep into the world of government information, beneath the home pages of websites both well-known and unknown, and we have brought to the surface the most informative, the most enlightening, and the most powerful tools that Uncle Sam has to offer.

Click on.

Notes to the Reader

Note 1. Before we get to these and hundreds of other treasures in Uncle Sam's domain, a few words about government information.

In 1976, I moved from Cambridge, Massachusetts, to Washington, D.C. to work for a book publishing company. I quickly learned that it was wrong to think of Washington as solely the political capital of America. A good friend related to me a syllogism that explains what I mean. He had been a high-ranking official at the Federal Trade Commission during the Carter Administration and was heading back to Cambridge to teach at Harvard. I asked him to explain the difference between the two cities. "If the currency of Cambridge is ideas," he said, "and the currency of New York is money, then the currency of Washington is a combination of information and power."

The power of information—that is as close to the mantra of our times as you're likely to get. I learned that Washington is more properly the "information capital" of the world; that the 3 million people who work for Uncle Sam nationwide are misnamed; that the word "bureaucrat" is misleading, because a "bureaucrat" is truly an "information specialist"; that civil servants spend their days and, even more likely, their careers devoted to the gathering of information on sometimes the narrowest or most esoteric subjects imaginable.

Three years later, when I became a literary agent, my first notion was to develop a book that could "tie a ribbon" around all the information sources in the federal government, to produce "the information book for the information age." I then met up with a man who had started a very successful company that served as a bridge between companies that wanted statistical information and the information specialists themselves. His name was Matthew Lesko, and Matthew went on to repackage *The U.S. Government Manual*—the best-selling book issued annually by the Office of the Federal Register at The National Archives—which told readers how to access any government agency or official to find out information on nearly any subject under the sun. We called his book *Information U.S.A.*, and it became a major national best-seller.

Most of all, I learned that this information belonged to me—to us. Politicians are forever saying that once WE elect THEM, THEY will fully serve US. We rarely believe them, of course, which is one of many reasons we have come to look cynically at anything that is derived from government.

But I look at Washington differently, not as a city of politicians but as the most comprehensive storehouse of knowledge and resource tools in the country. Think of the 16 million books and 91 million "other" items at the Library of Congress, such as rare manuscripts, movies, maps, manuscripts, and musical compositions. Think of the 4 billion pieces of paper and 7 million still photographs at the National Archives; the 91 million acres administered by the National Park Service and another 191 million acres maintained by the Agriculture Department. Think of the National Weather Service and the Patent Office and the National Institutes of Health. It sounds corny, but these belong to you. They exist because your taxes have paid for them. And now, in this still inchoate world of telecommunications, they are just a computer, a modem, and a fingertip away.

Note 2. Imagine that a new housing development was built across the freeway from you last year, and a number of friends and acquaintances have moved in over the past few months. The main street signs have been installed, but side streets are still being paved and street numbers have not even been fully posted. You drive over and find Main Street, but you can't find Elm Street or Maple Street because the county hasn't even printed a map.

The Internet is very much like that housing development, and the analogy certainly holds true for Uncle Sam's domain. Over the months of research on this book, a lot of "street signs" were going up, addresses were changing, agencies were converting from "gopher" pages to websites, home pages were being redesigned, and new sites were being added—literally, every day.

The Great American Web Book is, then, a work in progress. We've not tried to be comprehensive to the point of including every home page of every cubbyhole of the government. Frankly, they're not all gems or intimately involved with the lives of most Americans; or, the websites are still under construction, so it would be premature to include them here.

Following our organizational model, *The U.S. Government Manual,* we've first covered the government's three branches—legislative, judicial, and executive. Next come the executive agencies (cabinet departments) and independent establishments and government corporations (e.g., CIA, EPA, SEC). Lesser-known agencies of government may warrant inclusion in the next edition. In this First Edition, we've focused on those parts of government that we felt were immediately interesting to most readers and researchers and that had established an "online presence" on the Internet.

Note 3. For the reasons just cited, it's entirely possible that you may find a worthy home page to a government agency or a new website we've not uncovered. It's also quite possible that an address has changed or, God forbid, that we've made an error in an address that we can't blame on the copyeditor or proofreader. Again, *The Great American Web Book* is a work in progress, and we're eager to hear from you. Let us know if you find a new site that you think merits inclusion or consideration in a subsequent edition, and please let us know of an address change or if we goofed and left your hourglass or cursor hanging in cyberspace.

You can contact us at:

Inside Information
P.O. Box 30373
Bethesda, MD 20824
E-mail: UncleSam@cais.com

Note 4. Alas, we are not the first to take note of the treasures in Uncle Sam's domain. We urge you to consult these additional reference tools to access Uncle Sam.

Villanova's Federal Web Locator
http://www.law.vill.edu/Fed-Agency/fedwebloc.html

> Hats off to the Villanova Center for Law Information and Policy. Its Federal Web Locator, a comprehensive guide to government websites, roughly follows, as we do, the organization of *The U.S. Government Manual.* The Locator, which is updated frequently, connects to city, state, and international government sites.

National Technology Transfer Center's U.S. Government Information Sources Webpage
http://iridium.nttc.edu/gov_res.html

> An index to over 800 government webpages with an especially valuable search tool.

Yahoo
http://www.yahoo.com

Infoseek
http://www.infoseek.com

and

Lycos
http://www.lycos.com

> These are three of the best-known indexes that help you navigate the World Wide Web. They offer quick access to literally millions of websites, including those in the federal government. Their home pages cover broad topical areas, such as Arts, Business, Citizenship, and Government. Click on Government and you'll find a smorgasbord of the newer and better sites in Uncle Sam's domain.

The White House
http://www.whitehouse.gov/WH/html/handbook.html

> **The Interactive Citizens Handbook** at the White House site uses hypertext to link all of the executive departments

and many of the agencies and other government organizations that are online. The selection of organizations is not complete, but the site is extremely easy to navigate.

FedWorld
http://www.fedworld.gov

Once upon a time—actually just a few years ago—to get government information online, you had to dial a Washington, D.C. phone number to log onto a computer or computer network of BBSes, or bulletin boards. Each bulletin board had a different number, so separate calls were needed to access the Census Bureau, for example, or the Department of Veteran Affairs. One of the goals of FedWorld was to link all these BBSes over the Internet. These bulletin boards still exist, and remain accessible from FedWorld, to serve those people who do not have access to the Internet or World Wide Web. But FedWorld has broadened its mission and boasts a first-class site which is a gateway to information from a number of government agencies.

At the bottom of the home page, you'll find a subject list ranging from Aeronautics to Veterans Affairs; under "physics," for example, you can link immediately to more than a dozen physics-related sites, such as the National Institutes of Standards and Technology and the Fermi National Accelerator Laboratory.

One of the most notable sources of information at FedWorld is **World NewsConnection** (http://wnc.fedworld .gov). This is a subscription service that brings you time-sensitive information from thousands of foreign media sources. Search by topic (e.g., drugs, terrorism, politics, environment, health), by region, or look in the text of an article, then narrow your search by date. You'll get a list of articles, television, and radio reports; all are in English or have been translated into English and most contain the full text. The subscription fee, at this time, begins at $50/month for unlimited online searching.

Another key site is the **Federal Job Announcement Search** (http://www.fedworld.gov/jobs/jobsearch.html)

which offers daily listings of 1500 or more employment opportunities in government, updated at 9:30 A.M. every Tuesday through Saturday.

A division of the Commerce Department, **The National Technical Information Service** (http://www.fedworld.gov /ntis/ntishome.html), has an enormous number of products available through FedWorld, ranging from books to articles to audiovisual materials. NTIS is a "nonappropriated agency," meaning it relies on sales and subscriptions rather than on taxpayer revenue. Check the more complete listing in this book at the Department of Commerce.

Government Information Locator Service (GILS)
http://info.er.usgs.gov/gils/index.html

You'll see GILS, another search tool, referred to often throughout this book. Eventually, this tool will allow a user to search for and receive almost any type of government information. So far, only a few agencies (e.g., the Government Printing Office and the National Archives) have GILS sites and contribute to its large database of information. As more departments and agencies sign on, GILS will become a very powerful central source of information.

Before You Begin

All you need are a computer, a modem, and an Internet provider. But what kinds and types? We did our research primarily on a mail-order Gateway computer with a Pentium 100 microchip, a 28.8 modem, and a Netscape Navigator 2.0 browser. The speedier fax modem (as opposed to the 14.4, which we used at first) is especially important since downloading nontextual material can be a slow, arduous process. In just the last six months of 1995, off-the-shelf computer systems have moved from a 14.4 to 28.8 fax modem standard, and it's entirely possible that a new standard, such as ISDN (Integrated Services Digital Network) or digital telephone lines, will be in place by 1997. In short, the faster the modem speed, the faster photographs and other visual images will appear on screen, and the more satisfying your online experience will be.

The last key question is Internet access. Online services like America Online, Prodigy, and Compuserve can set you up with a low-maintenance, easy-to-use connection. If you're a novice navigator of cyberspace, we recommend you talk with friends and colleagues to find out what their service provider might be. You'll want to consider a high-performance connection through a local Internet provider. Names of local providers should be easily retrievable from a computer dealer or in the business and technology section of your newspaper. Our thanks to our local provider, Capital Area Internet Service, for its consistently good connections.

Understanding Addresses in Uncle Sam's Domain

Because this book is primarily an address book, it's fairly important to speak the language of government electronic communications and to know the difference between "www" and "gopher" or "telnet" and the like.

The first acronym to know is the URL, or Universal Resource Locator, which is essentially an Internet address. The URL for the **Library of Congress,** for example, is (http://www.loc.gov); think of it as the equivalent of the complete address for your home or apartment: street name and number, apartment number, and zip code. Like all Internet addresses, URLs are rather precise. If you misread or mistype a letter, period, semicolon, or backslash, you are not likely to make the connection.

Type the URL, exactly as it appears, into the address space provided on your web browser, and you will be connected to the home page of the agency, department, or organization you chose.

Most URLs begin with a set of introductory letters and typographical items that look like this: **http://.** Sites that begin with this designation, which stands for Hypertext Transport Protocol, are traditional pages on what we think of as the World Wide Web, with graphics, text, and the ability to be linked to other pages by hypertext links. Web pages are the most eye-pleasing and user-friendly sites your web browser will be able to access.

You'll encounter two other types of addresses: **gopher** and **FTP** (File Transfer Protocol). These older sites are immediately recognizable because their URL begins with those letters. They were the primary means of accessing and organizing information on the Internet before web pages came along. Both look like "file cabinets" on your web browser screen. You'll see folders that hold documents, programs, files, or other information. Although not as user-friendly as web pages, gopher and FTP sites are valuable ways to retrieve government information for those with the patience to spend time searching through them. Examples of useful gopher services are **LC MARVEL** at the Library of Congress (gopher://marvel.loc.gov) and the **State Department** gopher (gopher://dosfan.lib.uic.edu).

The fourth type of site accessible from your web browser, the telnet site (designated in a URL by "**telnet://**"), is somewhat different. Many of what are now called telnet sites have been around for ten or more years and were originally government Bulletin Board Systems (BBSes). Telnet sites are text-only, have no graphics capabilities, and are gradually being supplanted by the more graphics-oriented technologies. Many are still extremely useful and should not be ignored just because they are more difficult to use. The best examples of government telnet sites are the **Veterans Affairs BBS, VA Online** (telnet://vaonline.va.gov), and the Library of Congress **LOCIS** system (telnet://locis.loc.gov).

Some web browsers need an extra piece of software in order to access telnet sites. The best way to find out whether you need this additional software is to try to visit a telnet site and see what happens. If your web browser is configured to use telnet software, a window should pop open and prompt you to log in to a computer. You must do this in order to access the site.

Reading the Address

The URL often tells you quite a bit about the site that you are accessing. Take, for example, the URL for the National Weather Service website:

http://www.nws.noaa.gov

The **http** and **www** say this is a web page on the Internet (World Wide Web). The **nws** says you're at a site of the National Weather Service, one of the divisions of the National Oceanic and Atmospheric Administration **noaa** (itself part of the Commerce Department). And gov means this is an official government site. Most of the sites in this book will end in .gov or .mil (for military). Any of the other common domains—"com" (commercial), "org" (nonprofit organization), "edu" (educational institution), or "net" (network)—indicate either government sponsorship or simply a thematic link to a private website. For example, the sixteen clearinghouses at the Educational Research Information Center (ERIC) at the Department of Education are sponsored by the Department's Office of Education Research and are generally situated at universities around the country.

The informal rule about URLs is: The farther to the right you move, the more specific they become. Think of the example address in these terms: This is a web page (http://) on a World Wide Web site (www) that belongs to the National Weather Service (.nws), which is a part of the National Oceanic and Atmospheric Administration (.noaa), which is a part of the U.S. government (.gov).

If an address has a backslash (/) after the .gov, it means that you are accessing a directory within the designated address. Let's try another example:

http://www.ustreas.gov/treasury/bureaus/atf/atf.html

This is the address for the **Bureau of Alcohol, Tobacco, and Firearms,** an agency within the Treasury Department. The computer in use for this address is the main Treasury web server (www.ustreas.gov). But the ATF does not have its own true website. Instead, it has a directory on the main computer. Thus, /treasury/bureaus/atf/atf.html describes the location on this computer where you can find the ATF files. The URL would read: This is a webpage (http://) on a World Wide Web site (www) on the Treasury Department computer system (.ustreas), which is part of the government (.gov); we are accessing the treasury files (/treasury) and looking under the bureaus section (/bureaus) for the ATF (atf/atf.html).

That is the general thought process behind the addressing of URLs. Not every address conforms to these rules, but if you use these two examples as your guide, the web addresses should become a little easier to understand.

THE GREAT AMERICAN AMERICAN WEB BOOK

★ ★ ★

LEGISLATIVE BRANCH

★ ★ ★

THE HOUSE OF REPRESENTATIVES

http://www.house.gov

"Write a letter to your Representative!" has long been the rallying cry of community coalitions, interest groups, and activists of all causes who want to let their House members know how they feel about any issues of the day. Now, with the rise of the World Wide Web, sending a message to Washington has never been easier. Most if not all Congress-people, in both the House and Senate, have both e-mail addresses and home pages, which are accessible through addresses cited below.

And there's much more. At the House website, you can learn all about pending bills, the making of laws, the difference between statutes and continuing resolutions, mark-ups and other minutiae of the legislative process.

The Legislative Process

http://www.house.gov/Legproc.html

Here's where you can read the full text and current status of bills introduced into the House. The **House Votes** section lets you find immediately the tally pro and con, and how each member voted. Search by bill number or by words that describe the purpose of the measure. Click on **Tying It All Together** to get a complete overview of how a bill becomes a law.

3

Legislative

Who's Who
http://www.house.gov/Whoswho.html

The House is comprised of 435 Representatives from 50 states, plus a Resident Commissioner from Puerto Rico, and Delegates from American Samoa, the District of Columbia, Guam, and the Virgin Islands. Phone numbers and addresses are provided in the **Member Directory.** E-mail addresses of the Representatives are cited on a separate page. You can also contact all the Committees of the current Congress, some of which have e-mail addresses as well.

Organization and Operations
http://www.house.gov/Orgops.html

The complete text of Thomas Jefferson's *Manual of Parliamentary Practice* is featured, as well as the text of the House *Ethics Manual.* Organizational charts show the makeup of the House leadership and administration.

Member Information
http://www.house.gov/Orgpubs.html

There are three types of information here. Most useful are the **Member Pages,** where you'll find websites of individual members, with biographies, lists of press releases and newsletters, texts of sponsored legislation, and links to home-district information. The **Committee Pages** offer summaries of major legislation (and links to the text), membership lists, rules, hearing schedules (with links to subcommittee sites), and committee member biographies. At the **House Leadership Pages,** you'll find the House Republican Conference, Democratic Caucus, and hot-topic proposals—for example, the flat tax proposal.

Internet Law Library
http://law.house.gov

An extremely comprehensive site covering all U.S. federal laws, state laws, laws of other nations, treaties, and international law. Includes a searchable version of the U.S. Code and the Code of Federal Regulations. Enter in any subject or term and the programs will search through a database of all of the laws that mention your search term. Lawyers and students will find a useful set of links to legal professional directories and reviews of law books.

Visitor Information
http://www.house.gov/Visitor.html

Find out how you can attend a House session while visiting Washington. Also included: a description of available tours, a map of the Capitol, and a map of the Washington metro system.

Educational Resources
http://www.house.gov/Educat.html

The full text of the Declaration of Independence and the Constitution and Bill of Rights, as well as the text of amendments that were not ratified.

THOMAS
http://thomas.loc.gov

A central source of information about the entire legislative branch. See the full entry under Library of Congress (p. 17).

THE SENATE
http://www.senate.gov

The Senate website is less comprehensive than its House counterpart, though you have the same access to mailing and e-mail addresses, organized by name or by state. **The Legislative Process** explains filibusters and cloture, unanimous consent agreements, and other parlance of the Senate floor. For further information about bills, amendments, and schedules, go to THOMAS.

Directory of Senators
by name: http://www.senate.gov/senator/members.html
by state: http://www.senate.gov/senator/state.html

Search the alphabetical or state listings for any senator. Each listing has a photo, a biography, an address, an e-mail address when available, and a list of congressional committees and subcommittees on which the Senator serves or has served.

Senate Standing Committees
http://www.senate.gov/committee/committee.html

Each of the full, select, joint, and special committees is described. Also available: links to the pages of committee members, and a listing of subcommittees.

Visiting the U.S. Senate
http://www.senate.gov/tour/tour.html

Valuable information to prepare you for a visit to the Capitol in person; learn, for example, how to find Senators' offices (Hart, Dirksen, or another building? Room number?). Especially useful is the **Congressional Special Services Office** (CSSO) for disabled visitors (http://www.senate.gov/tour/csso.html), which provides guided tours, wheelchairs, interpreters, and other services. For further info on CSSO, call (202) 224-4048. You'll also enjoy a **Virtual Tour of the Capitol** (http://www.senate.gov/capitol/virtour.html), which offers a slide show featuring the Capitol Dome, the Rotunda, Statuary Hall, and other historic rooms.

United States Capitol
http://www.aoc.gov

Learn about the history of the Capitol building, the architects who designed it, and its works of art.

The Ten Best Agencies or Departments in Uncle Sam's Domain

1. Department of Commerce
2. NASA
3. Smithsonian Institution
4. Department of Health and Human Services
5. Library of Congress
6. Department of the Interior
7. Department of Defense
8. Department of State
9. The White House
10. Environmental Protection Agency

Legislative *(sidebar)*

GENERAL ACCOUNTING OFFICE
http://www.gao.gov

The General Accounting Office (GAO), the investigative arm of Congress, audits the use of federal money and evaluates government programs and activities. The reports of the Comptroller General, the head of the GAO, are posted here daily. You can search the database for past findings and you can subscribe to the GAO Daybook Mailing List through an online e-mail form. The best-seller list of GAO reports includes: (1) School Facilities: Conditions of America's Schools; (2) Information Superhighway: An Overview of Technology Challenges; (3) Cholesterol Measurement: Test Accuracy and Factors That Influence Cholesterol Levels; (4) Electric Vehicles: Likely Consequences of U.S. and Other Nations' Programs and Policies; and (5) Managing for Results: State Experiences Provide Insights for Federal Management Reforms.

Uncle Sam's National Libraries

The National Agricultural Library
(http://www.nalusda.gov)

The National Library of Education
(http://www.ed.gov/NLE)

The National Library of Medicine
(http://www.nlm.nih.gov)

The National Transportation Library
(http://www.bts.gov/smart/smart.html)

GOVERNMENT PRINTING OFFICE

http://www.access.gpo.gov

Over 430,000 documents, books, and brochures are produced each
year by the Government Printing Office (GPO). They can be ordered by
mail, telephone, or fax, or purchased through twenty-four U.S. government bookstores.

GPO Access

http://www.access.gpo.gov/su_docs/aces/aaces001.html

This is your entry point to online information in the GPO bookstore and
warehouse. Connect to **Online Databases,** scroll the display screen,
and you'll be able to access electronically any and all congressional
bills and documents of the current Congress, plus the *Federal Register,*
which is the daily log of all government activities. Two of the most useful and best-selling publications are the *Congressional Directory* and
The U.S. Government Manual (see below). GPO Access consolidates
information about web and gopher sites offered by the federal government. The University of California at San Diego has developed a first-
rate site, **GPO Gate** (http://ssdc.ucsd.edu/gpo), that accesses the same
information in an even more user-friendly way.

United States Government Information

http://www.access.gpo.gov/su_docs/sale/asale001.html

Your gateway to all publications, subscriptions, and CD-ROMs printed
by the GPO. Under **Publications,** your options include either an
alphabetical listing of the voluminous source materials, or a topical
bibliography. Try the latter, and the first eleven listings will be:
Accident Prevention, Accidents, Accounting, Adolescence, Aeronautics, Aerospace, Africa, African-Americans, Aging, Agriculture,
and AIDS. Under **Subscriptions,** the subject index begins with

Acquisition (Federal), Administrative Law, Air Traffic Control, Alcoholism, and Assistance (Federal). All these materials can be ordered from the GPO, or from **The United States Government Bookstore** (http://www.access.gpo.gov/su_docs_/sale/abkst001.html) where a clickable map shows the address, hours, phone and fax numbers of twenty-four bookstores around the country.

One of the key links here is to the **Consumer Information Center** (CIC) catalog, the source of thousands of free and low-cost publications. See the listing under the **General Services Administration,** which maintains the CIC's activities (p. 127).

NARA Office of the Federal Register
http://www.access.gpo.gov/nara/index.html

This unit of the National Archives and Records Administration is devoted to publications of the National Archives materials, including the perennial GPO best-seller, *The U.S. Government Manual,* the indispensable official handbook of the federal government, which is now online and completely searchable. Compiled annually, the *Manual* has complete descriptions of all agencies, bureaus, and departments and their programs, and lists their principal officials' names, addresses, and telephone numbers. (*The U.S. Government Manual* does not yet contain website addresses, which is in part the inspiration for this book.) See the entry for the National Archives and Records Administration (p. 152).

Government Information Locator Service
http://www.access.gpo.gov/su_docs/gils/gils.html

Still can't find material on certain subjects? GILS will help you access many federal information systems. The records in the GPO's GILS database are provided by more than three dozen individual agencies including:

Department of State

Office of Personnel Management

Federal Reserve Board

Pension Benefits Guaranty Corporation

Federal Trade Commission

Selective Service Administration

Social Security Administration

Department of Commerce

Department of the Treasury

General Services Administration

Office of Management and Budget

Most Conspicuously Absent Official Websites

U.S. Supreme Court

U.S. Surgeon General

LIBRARY OF CONGRESS
http://www.loc.gov

What if you could access by computer, from your own home, the complete contents of the vast storehouse of knowledge situated at the Library of Congress? The possibilities are staggering—millions of documents, books, films, photos, and other artifacts, perhaps the greatest gathering of intellectual property in the world.

It is the Library's mission, in the words of its Librarian, James Billington, to preserve, secure, and sustain both "a comprehensive record of American history and creativity" and "a universal collection of human knowledge." Toward that end, the Librarian has a grand ten-year mission to make all these materials available to everyone through the Internet. Although only a fraction of this storehouse is now online, the Library of Congress (LOC) is a monumental website. In a span of one year, the Copyright Office has gone online, as has an extraordinary electronic exhibit about the Declaration of Independence. Another new addition is the **Global Legal Information Network** (http://lcweb2.loc.gov/glin/glinhome.html), providing a database of national laws from more than 35 countries. And, the **Motion Picture and Television Reading Room** (http://lcweb.loc.gov/rr/mopic) now features online films dating back to the turn of the century.

Like so many other developing sites, the home page does not readily reveal the riches underneath. Here are the highlights, though we urge you to return often and check the **What's New** page.

Library of Congress General Information
http://lcweb.loc.gov/homepage/genpub.html

An overview of LOC's website and some of its features, including information for the real-time visitor to the Library, an online *Thesaurus,* and selections from the handsome *Civilization* magazine. This is also your gateway to the Library's **Illustrated Guides,** featuring: Manuscripts; Music, Theater, and Dance; Prints and Photographs; and Rare Books and Special Collections.

Library of Congress Online Exhibits
http://lcweb.loc.gov/exhibits

Text and photos guide you through the electronic exhibitions on display. Three of the best are:

Declaring Independence: Drafting the Documents
http://lcweb.loc.gov/exhibits/declara/declara1.html

Letters and early drafts recreate the process by which Thomas Jefferson and John Adams and their cohorts wrote the Declaration of Independence. Be sure to read the little-known 1826 letter from Jefferson to one Roger C. Weightman, declining the invitation to attend the celebration of the 50th anniversary of American independence. The letter, which LOC calls "one of the sublime evaluations of individual and national liberty," reads, in part: "May it be to the world, what I believe it will be . . . the signal of arousing men to burst the chains under which monkish ignorance and superstition had persuaded them to bind themselves, and to assume the blessings and security of self-government." It is Jefferson's last known letter. He and Adams both died ten days later, on July 4, 1826, the 50th anniversary day.

Gettysburg Address
http://lcweb.loc.gov/exhibits/G.Address/ga.html

On November 2, 1863, a local judge named David Wills invited President Lincoln to attend the consecration of a Union cemetery for the war dead at Gettysburg. "[T]hese ceremonies," he wrote in a letter, now on display, "will doubtless be very imposing and solemnly impressive." Of the five known manuscript copies of the Address, delivered on November 19, 1863, the Library of Congress has two. President Lincoln gave one to each of his two secretaries, John Nicolay (this copy is often called "the first draft") and John Hay. Also on exhibit is the text of both the first draft and the final version highlighting the differences.

The African-American Mosaic
http://lcweb.loc.gov/exhibits/african/intro.html

The first LOC resource guide to the African-American collection. Online exhibits will expand considerably by the end of 1996. On our visit, we saw four areas covered, with stunning maps, posters, and drawings: Colonization, Abolition, Migration, and the Works Progress Administration (WPA).

Digital Library Collections
http://lcweb.loc.gov/homepage/digital.html

Devoted to collections that have been scanned or otherwise entered into the LOC computer database. So far, these are some of the sections accessible:

American Memory
http://lcweb2.loc.gov/amhome.html

This is a wonderful model of what an online museum can be. As an example, **Carl Van Vechten Photographs, 1932–1964,** is comprised of portraits of literary figures, celebrities, and other famous persons, including F. Scott Fitzgerald, Emma Goldman, Dizzy Gillespie, and Alfred A. Knopf. In **Life History Manuscripts from the Federal Writers' Project, 1936–1940,** you'll read the anonymous writings from a Great Depression-eraWPA project that helped launch the careers of writers like Saul Bellow, John Cheever, Ralph Ellison, and Zora Neale Hurston. An extraordinary exhibit centers on **Selected Civil War Photographs** (from the Prints and Photographs Collection) which were made under the supervision of Matthew Brady. Be sure to click on the **Time Line** for a brief year-by-year history of the Civil War, the text of which is drawn largely from the work of Richard B. Morris—in particular, his *Encyclopedia of American History.* The Time Line is interspersed with a few of the photos from the archives, including the Battle of the *Monitor* and the *Merrimac,* and Antietam, September–October 1862. The National Digital Library Program recently received a $1 million grant from Reuters America, Inc., and the Reuter Foundation to put digitalized versions of the papers of George Washington and Thomas Jefferson online; go to (http://lcweb2.loc.gov:8081 /ammem/GW) for a wonderful taste of what's to come.

Special Collections
http://lcweb.loc.gov/spcoll/spclhome.html

The rich tapestry of American history and culture will come alive in the Special Collections. Search the Library's collections by subject (Agriculture, History, Frontier Life, Popular Culture) and by state and regions. This site will introduce you to the vast collection (and how to access it when you're at the real Library).

Country Studies and Area Handbooks
http://lcweb.loc.gov/homepage/country.html

These books, produced jointly by the U.S. Army and the Library of Congress, outline the history, politics, culture, social structure, and government of approximately seventy countries.

LOC Online Services
http://lcweb.loc.gov/homepage/online.html

Here you'll learn of three important tools for navigating the riches of the Library of Congress. The first is **LOCIS**—the Library of Congress Information System—the most complete card catalog in the world, with over 27 million records located in a variety of databases. Many of the commands and search techniques are not user-friendly, and the Library is looking at state-of-the-art software to replace the system (see Z39.50, described on page 16).

You must Telnet into LOCIS to access the Main Library of Congress Catalog, where you'll find records for every book, map, film, piece of music, computer file, manuscript, poster, and recording registered with the Library. Look for a database that includes summaries of federal legislation, a complete file of copyright records registered since 1978, and a file containing abstracts and citations of foreign laws and regulations. One of the most useful files is the bibliography of 13,000 organizations that perform research in science, technology, and social science and can provide information to almost anyone.

Start with a simple search of LOCIS by title, subject, or author; once you've mastered the technique, you can move on to more complex searches. For instructions on how to use LOCIS, visit (gopher://marvel .loc.gov:70/11/locis/guides).

A more state-of-the-art tool is the Z39.50 system, a form-based system that will significantly ease your search through the Library. It's a powerful tool being used by more and more libraries, and it should eventually replace LOCIS as the best source of card catalog information. Visit **Z39.50 Gateway** at (http://lcweb.loc.gov/z3950), and you'll find complete operating instructions and a list of other similar servers.

The third tool, **LC MARVEL** (which stands for Machine Assisted Realization of the Virtual Electronic Library), is a huge file cabinet of government documents. As a gopher system, it is text-based and serves the vital function of linking you to most other gopher servers in other government departments and agencies. Check in at (gopher://marvel.loc .gov) for that extraordinary range of menu options. As of two years ago, LC MARVEL was state-of-the-art. It is still very useful.

Vietnam Era POW/MIA Database
http://lcweb2.loc.gov/pow/powhome.html

A collection of 121,764 records relating to prisoners of war and U.S. military personnel killed, missing, or imprisoned in Southeast Asia during or after the Vietnam War. Search the database by name, location, or any other relevant term to find documents relating to a person, place, or event in the LOC collection. Included are letters from POWs, reported sightings of POWs, and government documents and memos.

In addition, **Task Force Russia** is a storehouse of records about Americans believed to have been held in the former Soviet Union. It works the same way as the POW/MIA database.

THOMAS
http://thomas.loc.gov

Few websites have received as much media attention as THOMAS (as in Jefferson), the center for information about the legislative branch of government, inaugurated with much fanfare by House Speaker Newt Gingrich at the beginning of the 104th Congress.

What you can search at THOMAS: the full text of all House and Senate bills of the past few sessions of Congress; the full text of the *Congressional Record,* by speaker, topic, or date; and digests and legislative history of bills and amendments. One nice feature is THOMAS's version of a "hot list," that is, major bills receiving floor attention as selected by legislative analysts in the Congressional Research Service.

THOMAS has excellent links to other sites, including the House and Senate web servers listed elsewhere. One of the best is **C-SPAN** (http://www.c-span.org), which has started to use "RealAudio" to broadcast reports over the Internet. If you can download the RealAudio player, you can listen to these reports in real time as if you were using a CD player.

U.S. Copyright Office
http://lcweb.loc.gov/copyright

"To promote the progress of science and useful arts by securing for limited times to authors and inventors the exclusive right to their respective writings and discoveries."—U.S. Constitution, Article 1, Section 8. The Copyright Office is the authoritative source for everything you need to know about copyright laws and procedures. Learn how to protect your intellectual property by copyrighting your own work, whether it's a book, poem, game, musical composition, or piece of art, whether it's published or unpublished.

From the home page, click on **Copyright Basics** to learn the history and principles of copyright law; what works can be protected and what works cannot. At **Copyright Information Circulars,** access a dozen gopher documents that explain work-for-hire, fees, renewals, and more. Through **LOCIS,** search the records of the Copyright Office dating back to 1978. Newly online are downloadable **Copyright Application Forms** (http://lcweb.loc.gov/copyright/forms.html) for registering literary works, performing arts, sound recordings, and visual arts.

At **Internet Resources,** the Copyright Office reproduces U.S. Copyright Law Title 17 and offers links to copyright and intellectual property organizations such as BMI (Broadcast Music Incorporated), BSA (Business Software Alliance), and the National Writers Union. Also, learn about a project called **CORDS** (Copyright Office Electronic Registration, Recordation, and Deposit System) which should eventually allow for digitized copyright applications, although that link is likely months or years away.

American Folklife Center
http://lcweb.loc.gov/folklife

Created in 1976, this center for the study of American folk traditions incorporates the **Archive of Folk Culture** (founded in 1928). Use the LC MARVEL menu at the Folklife Archive to learn of the complete contents of the collection. One of LOC's internet resources, **Ethnographic Studies,** (http://lcweb.loc.gov/folklife/other.html) will link you to a score of resources in anthropology, ethnomusicology, folklore, and folklife.

National Library Service for the Blind and Physically Handicapped
http://lcweb.loc.gov/nls/nls.html

NLS provides free lending of recorded and braille books and other media through a network of cooperating libraries, all of which are linked at this site.

Resources for Greek and Latin Classics
http://lcweb.loc.gov/global/classics/classics.html

A guide to the classics collections at the Library of Congress, images from the "Rome Reborn" electronic exhibit, and an extraordinarily comprehensive list of links to other Greek and Latin classics resources on the Internet, including universities, associations, electronic journals, mailing lists, publishers' catalogs, and software.

Newspaper and Current Periodical Reading Room
http://lcweb.loc.gov/global/ncp/ncp.html

One of the great pleasures of any library is its reading room. Well, this is a reading room like no other. Pull up a chair and be prepared to spend a while, for you'll have immediate access to hundreds of newspapers, journals, and periodicals from all around the world. Here are just a few examples of the online links you'll find at (http://lcweb.loc.gov/global/ncp/oltitles.html):

United States Newspapers

Chicago Tribune, Dallas Morning News, Detroit Free Press, Miami Herald, Hartford Courant, Houston Chronicle, Knight-Ridder Daily Newspapers, New York Times Fax, Philadelphia Inquirer, St. Petersburg Times, San Francisco Chronicle, USA Today, + over 50 others.

Foreign Newspapers

Bermuda Sun, El Economista (Mexico), *Financial Times* (London), *The Hindu* (India), *Izvestia* (Russia), *Jerusalem Post* (Israel), *Jornal do Brasil* (Rio de Janeiro), *Kathmandu Post* (Nepal), *Liberation* (Paris), *Makedonia Thessaloniki* (Greece), *Malaysian News, La Nacion* (Costa Rica), *El Periodico de Catalunya* (Spain), *Pravda* (Bratislava, Slovakia), *La Republica* (Peru), *Singapore Business Times, Il Sole 24 Ore* (Italy), *Der Standard* (Vienna), *The Sunday Times Innovation* (London), *Die Welt* (Hamburg, Germany), + over 40 more.

Periodicals

Advertising Age, American Journalism Review, The Ancient History Bulletin, The British Medical Journal, Chronicle of Higher Education, Columbia Journalism Review, Condé Nast Traveler, The Economist, Fortune, The Internet Gazette, Internet World, Life, Mother Jones, NASDAQ, Financial Executive Journal, PC Magazine, The Popular Mechanics Zone, Sports Illustrated, Technology Review, + over 40 more.

Also linked from this website are a list of e-mail addresses for historical newspaper collections (Colonial Period, War of Independence, Presidencies of George Washington and Thomas Jefferson, and the Civil War), journalism schools, and journalism history.

Electronic Texts and Publishing Resources
http://lcweb.loc.gov/global/etext

A potpourri of literature, modern book publishing, and Internet resources. There is no specific LOC material at this site, but you'll be amazed at what links (mainly to university sites) you'll find. Under **Works by Specific Authors,** you can access and download the complete or nearly complete works of, at last count, eleven writers, including Shakespeare, Jane Austen, C.S. Lewis, Mark Twain, James Joyce, and Edgar Allan Poe. Under **Poetry Sites,** you'll find the works of Emily Dickinson, Shelley, Keats, and Wordsworth.

Library and Information Science
http://lcweb.loc.gov/global/library

Your gateway to libraries and library resources throughout the world, with links to:

National Library of Australia
http://www.nla.gov.au

National Library of Canada
http://www.nlc-bnc.ca

National Library of The Czech Republic, Prague
http://alpha.nkp.cz/welcome_eng.html

The Royal Library, Denmark
http://www.kb.bib.dk

National Library of Estonia
http://mercury.nlib.ee/index.html

National Library of Malaysia
http://www.pnm.my

National Library of France
http://web.culture.fr/culture/sedocum/bnf.htm

Norwegian National Library
http://mack.nbr.no/e_index.html

National Library of Spain
http://www.bne.es

Other offerings: **Indexes to Library Online Catalogs** and dozens of **Special Collections** (e.g., Oxford-Radcliffe Science Library, and Bodleian Library) and **Digital Library Activities** (e.g., at Stanford, Michigan, and Berkeley).

State and Local Governments

http://lcweb.loc.gov/global/state/stategov.html

LOC calls this a "Meta-index"—links to all fifty state government pages and a set of links to other state associations and government information.

Best Sites on Disasters

Asteroid and Comet Impact Hazard
(http://george.arc.nasa.gov/sst)

Cascades Volcano Observatory
(http://vulcan.wr.usgs.gov)

National Earthquake Information Center
(http://wwwneic.cr.usgs.gov)

National Hurricane Center
(http://www.nhc.noaa.gov)

National Landslide Information Center
(http://gldage.cr.usgs.gov/html_files/nlicsun.html)

Preparing for a Disaster
(http://www.fema.gov/fema/predis.html)

OFFICE OF TECHNOLOGY ASSESSMENT

RIP: The Office of Technology Assessment, created by Congress in 1972 to provide congressional committees with analyses of emerging and often technical issues, was closed in September 1995. Mirror sites containing its papers can be found in several locations, including one at the **National Academy Press** (http://www.ota.nap.edu) and another at the **Government Printing Office** (http://www.access.gpo.gov/ota).

★ ★ ★
JUDICIAL BRANCH
★ ★ ★

THE SUPREME COURT

http://www.law.cornell.edu/supct/supct.table.html

Less eager to announce itself than any other part of the U.S. government, the Supreme Court has no self-generated website at this time. We direct you instead to the Cornell University site, which features the **Decisions of the U.S. Supreme Court.** Search through a list of decisions from the past five years either by topic (such as "Abortion" or "Schools") or by any relevant term. Then read the case syllabus and the Court's opinion, including concurring, dissenting, and other opinions.

For the ongoing Supreme Court term, stay current by subscribing to a regular e-mail bulletin that summarizes court judgments as they are entered. You can also search decisions in the current term by month. The same choices are available for each previous term, individually, since 1990.

Also included are some highlight pages focusing on pre-1990 decisions about school prayer, copyrights, patent law, trademarks, and *Roe v. Wade*; a hypertext document that discusses the Federal Rules of Evidence; and a completely searchable list of the rules of the Supreme Court.

ADMINISTRATIVE OFFICE OF THE UNITED STATES COURTS
http://www.uscourts.gov

"The judicial power of the United States shall be vested in one supreme Court and in such inferior Courts as the Congress may from time to time ordain and establish."—Article III, U.S. Constitution.

This is the home page of the **U.S. Federal Courts,** maintained by the Administrative Office of the U.S. Courts, that serves as a clearinghouse for information about the federal judiciary system.

A hypertext document, **Understanding the Federal Courts,** describes how the U.S. Federal Courts operate. There are also selected articles from *The Third Branch,* the monthly newsletter of the federal courts.

FEDERAL JUDICIAL CENTER
http://www.fjc.gov

The Federal Judicial Center, the research and education arm of the federal court system, produces many studies and documents relating to federal court issues. A list of downloadable publications includes: "Reference Manual on Scientific Evidence," "Guideline Sentencing Update," and "Electronic Media Coverage of Federal Civil Proceedings." Also valuable are a telephone contact list, and links to the full text of the Federal Rules of Evidence and U.S. Supreme Court Rules, both of which are at the Cornell site given above (see Supreme Court listing).

THE UNITED STATES COURTS OF APPEALS
http://www.law.vill.edu/Fed-Ct/fedcourt.html#usappeals

Again, not an official government site, but The Federal Court Locator at
The Villanova Center for Information Law and Policy is your gateway to
the various circuit courts whose websites are located at different universities. Each has similar material, including the syllabus and summaries
of decisions for every recent case (within two or three years) and one or
more different ways to search through the decisions.

First Circuit
http://www.law.emory.edu/1circuit

Second Circuit
http://www.law.pace.edu/legal/us-legal/judiciary
/second-circuit.html

Third Circuit
http://www.law.vill.edu/Fed-Ct/ca03.html

Fourth Circuit
http://www.law.emory.edu/4circuit

Fifth Circuit
http://www.law.utexas.edu/us5th/us5th.html

Sixth Circuit
http://www.law.emory.edu/6circuit

Seventh Circuit
http://www.kentlaw.edu/7circuit

Eighth Circuit
http://www.wulaw.wustl.edu/8th.cir

Ninth Circuit
http://www.law.vill.edu/Fed-Ct/ca09.html

Tenth Circuit
http://www.law.emory.edu/10circuit

Eleventh Circuit
http://www.law.emory.edu/11circuit

D.C. Circuit
http://www.ll.georgetown.edu/Fed-Ct/cadc.html

Federal Circuit
http://www.ll.georgetown.edu/Fed-Ct/cafed.html

☆ ☆ ☆

EXECUTIVE BRANCH

☆ ☆ ☆

THE WHITE HOUSE

http://www.whitehouse.gov

One of the deservedly popular sites on Uncle Sam's web is an excellent introduction to the executive branch of government.

Executive Office of the President

http://www.whitehouse.gov/WH/EOP/html/couples.html

Here is where you'll find links to the home pages of the President, the Vice President, and the First Lady, each of which features a biography, recent speeches, and online e-mail forms. If your web browser cannot take advantage of the online forms, their addresses are as follows: president@whitehouse.gov, vice.president@whitehouse.gov, and first.lady@whitehouse.gov. The mailing address is: 1600 Pennsylvania Avenue, Washington, D.C. 20500. Phone: (202) 456-1414. Fax: (202) 456-2883.

Vice President Gore's ambition to "reinvent government" has led to the creation of the **National Performance Review** (http://www.npr.gov) which, in collaboration with the Lawrence Livermore National Laboratory, has its own page of reports and publications aimed at creating "a government that works better and costs less." A related page is **FinanceNet** (http://www.financenet.gov) which seeks to link public and private sector professionals in management and finance. Created early in 1996, the **U.S. Business**

Advisor (http://www.business.gov), promises to be "the one-stop electronic link to government for business." It's a first-rate site with links to federal government information, services, and transactions of special interest to small businesses and entrepreneurs.

A new White House site, the **Federal Statistics Briefing Rooms** (http://www.whitehouse.gov/fsbr), will speed your access to government statistics. The two "briefing rooms" arrange selected economic and social indicators by themes such as Output, Income, Employment, Education, Health and Crime, with hyperlinks to many of the pages cited above.

White House Offices and Agencies
http://www.whitehouse.gov/WH/EOP/html/EOP_org.html

There are 16 offices and agencies that are part of the Executive Office of the President accessible from this site, including the **Council of Economic Advisers,** the **Office of the First Lady** and the **President's Council on Physical Fitness and Sports.** Here are some of the others:

Office of Management and Budget
http://www.whitehouse.gov/WH/EOP/OMB/html/ombhome.html

A Citizen's Guide to the Budget assesses current budget proposals and **Budget Systems and Concepts Summary** tries to clarify the meaning of the proposals. Also, OMB regulations and miscellaneous publications with links to other sites of special interest to checkbook balancers.

Office of Science and Technology Policy
http://www.whitehouse.gov/WH/EOP/OSTP/html /OSTP_Home.html

Reports on everything from biotechnology to managing and disposing of plutonium. You can also subscribe to science-technology releases through the White House Publications Service.

Office of National Drug Control Policy
http://www.whitehouse.gov/WH/EOP/ondcp/html/ondcp.html

> A hypertext guide to the national drug control strategy
> (treatment, prevention, domestic law enforcement,
> interdiction, and international).

United States Trade Representative
http://www.ustr.gov

> An overview of U.S. trade policy.

White House Fellows
http://www.whitehouse.gov/WH/WH_Fellows/html/fellows1.html

> White House fellowships bring Americans to public service
> posts to learn firsthand about policy making and public
> administration. Browse its history, the kinds of assignments
> available, the eligibility requirements, and the online
> application.

The Corporation for National Service
http://www1.whitehouse.gov/WH/EOP/cns/html/cns-index.html

> This program engages Americans of all ages and background in ser-
> vice to their communities. Its three main components are AmeriCorps,
> Learn and Serve America, and the National Senior Service Corps.

White House History and Tours
http://www.whitehouse.gov/WH/glimpse/top.html

> Tours of the White House, the Old Executive Office Building, and
> the First Ladies' Garden of the White House, and a clickable map of
> Washington landmarks. Most interesting are the pages devoted to
> biographical sketches of each President and First Lady in American
> history.

Executive Branch

The Briefing Room

http://www.whitehouse.gov/WH/html/briefroom.html/

The next best thing to being in the White House press corps; read the press secretary's daily briefing and briefings of the past week.

The Ten Best Individual Websites in Uncle Sam's Domain

1. Views of the Solar System (Los Alamos)
   (http://bang.lanl.gov/solarsys)
2. NetCast (NOAA)
   (http://nic.noaa.gov/weather.html)
3. Planet Earth (DOD)
   (http://www.nosc.mil/planet_earth/info.html)
4. CIA World Factbook
   (http://www.odci.gov/cia/publications/95fact/index.html)
5. National AIDS Clearinghouse (CDC)
   (http://www.cdcnac.org)
6. U.S. Gazetteer (Census)
   (http://tiger.census.gov/cgi-bin/gazetteer)
7. American Memory (Library of Congress)
   (http://lcweb2.loc.gov/amhome.html)
8. Bureau of Consular Information (State)
   (http://travel.state.gov)
9. Visit Your National Parks (Interior)
   (http://www.nps.gov/parks.html)
10. Live from the Hubble Space Telescope (NASA)
    (http://quest.arc.nasa.gov/livefrom/hst.html)

Interactive Citizens Handbook

http://www.whitehouse.gov/WH/html/handbook.html

> One of the most useful sites at The White House—a gateway to valuable information in seven broad categories, among them Education and Training, Employment, and Health and Housing. Each of these pages provides additional links to dozens of topic-specific websites in and out of government. For example, Education and Training directs you to the education resources pages of NASA and the Departments of Education and Defense, the National Institute of Literacy, an Index of Colleges and Universities, and more. See those specific departments in this book for fuller explanation of the sites.

White House Virtual Library

http://www.whitehouse.gov/WH/html/library.html

> Search the White House database for all public documents released since the incumbent President took office, including all Executive Orders and all Sunday Radio addresses on an audio link. You can browse the contents of the Declaration of Independence, the Constitution, the North American Free Trade Agreement, and the General Agreement on Tariffs and Trade, and even subscribe to the daily publications mailing list.

White House for Kids

http://www.whitehouse.gov/WH/kids/html/kidshome.html

> A recent issue of the quarterly newsletter, Inside the White House, introduces future taxpayers to the economy, the deficit, and the budget. Kids, you can also send a brief message to the President or the First Lady. Use the convenient online form and you're assured you'll get a response!

Executive Branch

DEPARTMENT OF AGRICULTURE

http://www.usda.gov

> Among USDA's many missions are the maintenance and improvement of farm income, and the expansion of foreign markets for U.S. agricultural products. USDA aspires to curb and cure poverty, hunger, and malnutrition through food programs, even as it enhances America's great natural resources. The department is home to the U.S. Forest Service, whose responsibilities encompass 30 percent of Uncle Sam's land area.

Forest Service

http://www.fs.fed.us

> Your gateway to the 191 million acres that comprise the national forests. A clickable map of the entire country (http://www.fs.fed .us/recreation/map.htm) lets you discover forests close to you. Each entry includes scenic views (waterfalls and overlooks), descriptions of facilities, and information about fishing, camping, and other available activities. I clicked on the **George Washington and Jefferson National Forest** near my home and learned that it covers nearly 1.9 million acres in Virginia and West Virginia and has fifty campgrounds and 2,000 miles of hiking trails. Phone and fax numbers give easy access to follow-up information.
>
> Find out how to order individual forest maps which show roads, trails, campgrounds, and recreational facilities. For campground

reservations and fees, call (800) 280-CAMP (2267) or, to access individual forest areas and make reservations, go to (http://www.fs.fed.us /recreation/campres.htm) where you'll find the names, addresses, and local numbers of foresters throughout the nation.

National Agriculture Library
http://www.nalusda.gov

A huge collection of agriculture-related resources including access to ten information centers ranging from aquaculture to biotechnology to water quality. Dozens of online publications are available at the **Food and Nutrition Information Center** (http://www.nalusda.gov /fnic), the authoritative source of food composition and information about nutrition and food composition. Besides explaining how to read and interpret the new food label for processed foods, meat, and poultry, the Center tries to demystify and explain foodborne illnesses and how to prevent them. Read the online version of **Dietary Guidelines for Americans,** which provides links to other nutrition resources.

Natural Resources Conservation Service
http://www.ncg.nrcs.usda.gov

Formerly the Soil Conservation Service, NRCS advises farmers, ranchers, and others on how to develop conservation programs that preserve the land, water, vegetation, and habitats of America. The **Technical References** page (http://www.ncg.nrcs.usda.gov/tech_ref.html) has a searchable guide to its Conservation Practice Standards. For contractors doing maintenance or construction work, the National Engineering Handbook is online as well.

Horticulturists will have a field day with the wonderfully interactive **Plants Database** (http://plants.usda.gov:80/plants), which aims to be the "single source of standardized information about plants," including names, symbols, and other plant-related facts. Be sure to stop by the **Photo Gallery,** which is just one of many notable sites here. This is the authoritative source of plant information for the U.S. Forest Service, the Environmental Protection Agency, the National Park Service, and the Smithsonian Institution.

Agricultural Marketing Service

http://www.usda.gov/ams/titlepag.htm

Provides current information to producers, processors, distributors, and others, on supply and demand, prices, movement, product quality and condition, and other market data on farm products.

Foreign Agricultural Service

http://www.usda.gov/fas

Up-to-date reports from overseas bureaus about food crops around the world and import/export opportunities, including a database of foreign buyers, sorted by country and product, for agricultural products exporters.

Farm Service Agency

http://www.fsa.usda.gov

Access to agricultural reference materials on the agency's bulletin boards, and links to regional weather reports which have special impact on farms and farming.

Food and Consumer Service

http://www.usda.gov/fcs/fcs.htm

WIC, Food Stamps, the National School Lunches Program, and twelve other food assistance programs that serve one out of six Americans are administered by USDA's Food and Consumer Service program. At **Team Nutrition** (http://www.usda.gov/fcs/team.htm), the School Meals Initiative has tips for school personnel and parents about how to cook healthy meals for children.

The Carl Hayden Bee Research Center

http://gears.tucson.ars.ag.gov

A wonderful page for kids. The mission of this research center, known as GEARS (which stands for Global Entomology Agriculture Research Server) and located in Tucson, Arizona, is to improve crop pollination and bee productivity through the study of honey bee behavior. Multimedia exhibits feature a queen bee piping inside her hive and insect movies. Learn how to bee-proof your property and avoid stings.

National Agricultural Statistics Service

http://www.usda.gov/nass

Numbers, statistics, and reports about food, commodities, and land usage. Excellent graphics display the range and yield of all major agricultural crops, and links to state statistical offices.

Animal and Plant Health Inspection Service

http://www.aphis.usda.gov

The Animal and Plant Health Inspection Service is responsible for guarding against and monitoring domestic agricultural and animal diseases and pests. Learn about biological controls and pest management to combat the Mediterranean fruit fly, other pests, and noxious weeds. Results of the latest safety studies of genetically engineered plants are available.

DEPARTMENT OF COMMERCE
http://www.doc.gov

The government shutdown of late 1995–early 1996 underscored the significance of the Department of Commerce (DOC). There was no gathering of housing starts or retail sales, no publication of *Commerce Business Daily,* no up-to-date record of international sales. While most will know that DOC is the home of the Census Bureau, it's startling to realize how many more aspects of our lives are aided by the work of DOC, including the National Oceanic and Atmospheric Administration, the International Trade Administration, and the Patent and Trademark Office. Any businessperson can benefit from the voluminous data maintained, but there are many interesting sites for students, weather enthusiasts, map lovers, and researchers in any field. A good place to help navigate your search is at the DOC contents page (http://www.doc.gov/agencies.html).

Census Bureau
http://www.census.gov

A division of the Economics and Statistics Administration, Census is your gateway to DOC's on-line electronic services, especially the subscription service, **STAT-USA.** Other features include links to regional and state census bureaus, and a number of terrific tools like the **TIGER Mapping Service** and the **Thematic Maps.** The pages of the Census Bureau are updated continuously, so check often for new material.

Census Data Lookup
http://www.census.gov/cdrom/lookup

Here are the enormous data sets of the Census Bureau; use them to find smaller data subsets on almost any topic. You'll find official statistical data for 1,078 U.S. cities and all 3,141 counties as well as 11,097 places of 2,500 or more inhabitants. The home page looks daunting at first, but begin entering your choices and you'll soon learn how to create all the data combinations you want.

U.S. Gazetteer
http://www.census.gov/cgi-bin/gazetteer

If you know either the city/town or the zip code of your research point, this is an especially efficient tool to use to find your data, especially in conjunction with TIGER (see below).

TIGER Mapping Service
http://tiger.census.gov

If you use maps in your business research or classroom reports or if you simply want to have some fun with a new gizmo, you'll love the Topographically Integrated Geographic Encoding and Referencing System. TIGER allows you to create a map of any part of the United States, zooming in and out of your target, marking special areas with colored pushpins, entering Latitude and Longitude markers, and/or downloading it to your own computer to use in reports and presentations. Click on **Tiger 2.0 Version** and you'll see all these options. Be sure to use the Search function at the bottom of the page. I typed in my hometown of Springfield, MA and found the U.S. Gazetteer 1990 census, with a gateway to the TIGER map of Springfield and STF1A and STF3A tables to give me a remarkably comprehensive demographic profile of the city broken out by dozens of categories. The service can be slow, but patience pays off. For instructions on how to download the map you've created, read the information at (http://tiger.census.gov/instruct.html).

STAT-USA

http://www.stat-usa.gov

A powerful reference tool for business. Drawing upon the work of more than 50 federal agencies and a database of over 300,000 reports and series (the equivalent of seven sets of encyclopedias), discover market trends and use statistics to target potential business more effectively. What makes STAT-USA so effective is that it provides up-to-date economic news and market intelligence. (Most online census data, useful as it is, comes from the 1990 Census.) To use the full service, which accesses the National Trade Data Bank and the Economic Bulletin Board, a subscription fee is required (approx. $100 per year). It includes current information about exports, domestic trends in education, health, the environment, economy and criminal justice, analyses of markets and trends, and the Global Business Opportunities Service (GLOBUS), designed to help American businesses find procurement opportunities around the world. GLOBUS is also home to the *Commerce Business Daily.* You can take STAT-USA on a test drive with its sample database search, but don't expect to gain a lot from the free search. For further information, call the Helpline at 202-482-1986 or send e-mail to stat-usa@doc.gov.

You may also be interested in the **U.S. Budget Site** (gopher://gopher.stat-usa.gov:70/11/Budget FY96), which contains everything you ever wanted to know about the national budget. You're welcome to download the entire budget and try to balance it yourself.

The Statistical Abstract

http://www.census.gov/stat_abstract

The online version of The Statistical Abstract—Uncle Sam's official government almanac—culls the best and most useful statistics from all of the government agencies. Very similar to many commercial almanacs in breadth and depth (in fact, most commercial almanacs use some of the statistics found in this book), but with a focus on government statistics. The entire book is not online; for that you have to order the CD-ROM or buy the print version of the Abstract which can be done online. But you can get state rankings, statistics data in brief, and the most frequently requested tables. Under **Monthly Economic Indicators,** for example, you can access this data: Retail Trade, Wholesale Trade, Building Permits and Housing Starts, New Home Sales, Manufacturing, Foreign Trade, Money Supply, Consumer and Price Indexes, Civilian Labor Force and Unemployment.

Latest Statistical Briefs on Social and Demographic Topics

http://www.census.gov/socdemo/www

As the name of this site implies, an excellent overview focusing on many of the most highly requested subjects such as poverty and aging. In the section, "Sixty-Five Plus in the U.S.," we learned that the "oldest old," that is, age 85 and over, is the most rapidly growing elderly age group. Another discovery was the **Population Division Home Page** (http://www.census.gov/population/www) which is one-stop research for a population profile of the United States in 1995 and for population projections for the future. Still another was **Marital Status and Living Arrangements** (http://www.census.gov/population/www/ms-la.html), where we learned that over 3.5 million couples that live together are not married, and over one-third of these couples have children, and that almost 18 million children live with only one parent. A fun site is the set of U.S. and world **Pop Clocks** (http://www.census.gov/main/www /popclock.html) which keep track of the earth's population to the exact second using a population projection system. Try reloading the screen after a few seconds and you'll see how quickly the population increases. (At the **World Clock,** you can even get a chart of births and deaths and "natural increases" calculated to the year, month, day, hour, minute, and second.)

WWW Thematic Mapping System
http://www.census.gov/themapit/www

A geographic, data-visualization tool that allows you to create your own chart from among 3,000 data items (e.g., vital statistics, retail trade, poverty, health, housing, income, crime), and download your self-generated map.

Genealogy Information
http://www.census.gov/genealogy/www

A fee-based, age-search service will track census records back to 1910 and issue an official transcript of the results. Use these transcripts, which may have information on a person's age at the time of the census, place of birth, and relationship to household head, as evidence to qualify for social security, in making passport applications, to prove relationship in settling estates, and in genealogy research.

Name Frequency Database
http://www.census.gov/genealogy/www/freqnames.html

You'll love to visit the **Name Frequency Database** to find out the most—and least—popular first and last names according to the 1990 census.

Most Popular Names

Boys	*Girls*
James	Mary
John	Patricia
Robert	Linda
William	Barbara
David	Elizabeth
Richard	Jennifer
Charles	Maria
Joseph	Susan
Thomas	Margaret
Christopher	Dorothy
Daniel	Lisa
Paul	Nancy
Mark	Karen
Donald	Betty

Less Popular Names	
Boys	*Girls*
Lynwood	Pilar
Lindsay	Charla
Jewel	Elissa
Jere	Tiffani
Hal	Tana
Elden	Paulina
Dorsey	Leota
Darell	Breenna
Broderick	Jayme
Alonso	Carmel

We typed out the first names in our office and came up with the following: Jenny (282); Chris (96); Ethan (528); Erika (298), and Raphael (616). Try the last name database, too, which contains 88,000 names.

Census Bureau Data Maps

http://www.census.gov/statab/www/profile.html

Another remarkable tool to dig deep into the statistical files of individual states and regions. Using the clickable map of the United States, we went to our home state (Maryland) which led to a state map of all counties, clicked on our home county where we were able to access data on business patterns and an economic profile using various tables.

Census State Data Centers

http://www.census.gov/sdc/www

A related service, which provides links to academic and nonprofit groups as well as state government agencies that serve the business community.

Market Place

http://www.census.gov/mp/www/index2.html

Your Census Bureau retailer where you can order product information on any of the bureau's books, CD-ROMS, surveys, maps, or diskettes.

Bureau of Economic Analysis

http://www.bea.doc.gov

> If Census is the nation's factfinder, then the Bureau of Economic Analysis is our national accountant, integrating an enormous volume of data to draw an overall picture of the nation's economic position. One of its most valuable tools is the monthly newsletter, *Survey of Current Business,* subscriptions are available in hard copy or via STAT-USA.

Minority Business Development Agency

http://www.doc.gov/agencies/mbda/index.html

> MBDA distributes an electronic bulletin with information for minority businesspeople about programs, groups, and local and national activities. Subscribe for free at the MBDA website.

International Trade Administration

http://www.ita.doc.gov

> ITA seeks to help U.S. businesses compete in the global marketplace. A gem of a site is **GEMS,** or the Global Export Market Information System (http://www.itaiep.doc.gov), which has two terrific online services. One is **BEMS,** or the Big Emerging Markets homepage which targets the following key potential trading partners: The Chinese Economic Area (China, Hong Kong, and Taiwan), India, South Korea, Mexico, Brazil, Argentina, South Africa, Poland, Turkey, and the Association of Southeast Asian Nations (ASEAN), which includes Indonesia, Brunei, Malaysia, Singapore, Thailand, the Philippines, and Vietnam, with links to export information on each. The other highlight is **BISNIS Online**—The Business Information Service for the Newly Independent States. If you do business in Russia or one of the newly independent states, you'll find scores of U.S. Embassy cables, country reports and market information here, such as daily exchange rates for the ruble and U.S. dollar.

National Oceanic and Atmospheric Administration
http://www.noaa.gov

Weather lovers rejoice! NOAA is best known as the home to the National Weather Service, the authoritative source of weather reports you receive everyday in various media. But NOAA is also home to the National Ocean Service, the National Marine Fisheries Service, and the National Climatic and Geophysical Data Centers.

There are a number of ways to access this weather data inside Uncle Sam, but one of NOAA's newest pages, called **NetCast,** stands above the rest. Simply type in a city and state and what appears is a stunningly attractive map of the region with short- and long-term forecasts. Bookmark this address—(http://nic.noaa.gov/weather.html)—for it's a weather bureau you'll return to time and again.

NetCast is only one of many activities at NOAA; go to the **Network Information Center** (http://nic.noaa.gov) which features the "NOAA Site of the Day." At NOAA's **Regional Offices** (http://nic.noaa.gov/regional_map.html) you'll find a map of the United States which leads you to more gems of this agency. Click on the North West Region, for example, and you'll access NOAA services such as the Pacific Marine Environmental Lab and the Alaska Fisheries Science Center.

Here are a few of the other highlights at this fine agency:

Environmental Research Laboratories
http://www.erl.noaa.gov

Use the clickable map to access one of the eleven labs which seek to improve the understanding of Earth, its oceans and inland waters, and the space environment. Don't miss the **Space Environment Center** (http://www.sel.noaa.gov) which features the daily weather forecast for space, highlighting unusual sunspot activity, checking geomagnetic field levels and x-ray flux as well as providing new charts, graphs, and photos.

National Weather Service
http://www.nws.noaa.gov

> Check out the snow cover maps, radar and satellite images, and the explanation of weather map symbols. At the **Interactive Weather Information Network** (http://iwin.nws.noaa.gov/iwin/main.html), choose from graphics or text to find out about flood, hurricane or thunderstorm warnings. Be sure to click on the stunning maps of the U.S. and the world. Yet more weather info can be found in the five regional offices of the NWS:

> **Eastern Region**
> http://www.nws.noaa.gov/eastern.HTM
>
> **Southern Region**
> http://www.nws.noaa.gov/southern.HTM
>
> **Western Region**
> http://ssd.wrh.noaa.gov/index.html
>
> **Central Region**
> http://www.crhnwscr.noaa.gov
>
> **Pacific Region**
> http://www.nws.noaa.gov/pr/pacific.HTM

Best Weather Pages

Air Weather Service
(http://infosphere.safb.af.mil/users/aws/public_www)

National Weather Service's Interactive Weather Information Network (IWIN)
(http://iwin.nws.noaa.gov/iwin/graphicsversion/main.html)

NetCast (http://nic.noaa.gov/weather.html)

Space Environment Laboratory's Weather in Space
(http://www.sel.bldrdoc.gov)

The GLOBE Program

http://www.globe.gov

> The acronym stands for Global Learning and Observations to Benefit the Environment, a worldwide network of students, teachers, and scientists. Its highlight is **The GLOBE Program for Kids** (http://globe.fsl.noaa.gov), a joint NASA-NOAA project and a powerful educational tool for teachers in which kids can formulate their own weather conditions and create a map or globe for instruction or entertainment. Over 2,700 schools in 32 countries have registered to participate in the program. For information on how your children or school can get involved, look here or send e-mail to info@globe.gov.

National Climatic Data Center

http://www.ncdc.noaa.gov

> Are you planning a vacation and want to know the average rainfall of your destination? Or building a factory and need specifications on temperature variation? The NCDC offers interactive graphs covering rainfall and temperature for any part of the world from 1900 to 1993.

El Niño Theme Page

http://www.pmel.noaa.gov/toga-tao/el-nino

> El Niño is a disruption of the ocean-atmosphere system in the tropical Pacific having important consequences for weather around the globe. This page explains what El Niño is and produces real-time maps, graphs, and weather-updates to keep you informed about the possible effects of El Niño.

National Marine Fisheries Service

http://kingfish.ssp.nmfs.gov

> This agency administers NOAA's programs in support of conservation and management of living marine resources. Access the regional research centers and be sure to spend a

minute listening to a mournful selection of **Whale Songs** (http://kingfish.ssp.nmfs.gov:80/songs.html).

National Centers for Environmental Prediction
http://www.ncep.noaa.gov

These nine centers, which include the **Space Environment Center** (http://www.sel.noaa.gov), the **Climate Prediction Center** (http://nic.fb4.noaa.gov) and the **Aviation Weather Center** (http://www.awc-kc.noaa.gov) produce meteorological and oceanographic information for the National Weather Service, the Air Force and the Federal Aviation Administration. Another center, formerly known as the National Hurricane Center, is now the **Tropical Prediction Center** (http://www.nhc.noaa.gov). The day we checked in, a new tropical storm was brewing off the coast of South America and had just been named. The TPC reports all weather advisories, describes how hurricanes are named, and surveys the deadliest hurricanes of the century.

Patent and Trademark Office
http://www.uspto.gov

What can be patented? Namely, "any new and useful process, machine, manufacture or composition of matter, or any new and useful improvement thereof." More than 170,000 applications are received every year. Everything you need to know to register for a patent or trademark is readily available—a description of the documents needed to file, filing fees, and details on how and where you find out if someone else has already patented your idea. Access the **Patent Bibliographic Database** (http://patents.cnidr.org:4242) which contains all patents dating back to 1976 through the Center for Networked Information Discovery and Retrieval. Also online: a list of thousands of federally registered Patent Attorneys.

From the USPTO home page, the **AIDS Patent Project** (http://app.cnidr.org) is your starting point for patents relating to

Acquired Immune Deficiency Syndrome. A remarkable link is the **HIV Sequence Database** at the Los Alamos National Lab in New Mexico (http://hiv-web.lanl.gov) where a group of molecular biologists and computer technicians collect and analyze genetic sequences of HIV and related series. Funding for that project is provided by NIH and DOE.

National Technical Information Service
http://www.fedworld.gov/ntis/ntishome.html

NTIS, the nation's largest central clearinghouse for scientific, technical, engineering, and other business-related information (with 2.7 million titles in its database), is maintained through FedWorld. NTIS operates solely on the revenue generated by sales of items in its collection. Among the subscription products: **NTIS Bibliographic Database** (http://www.fedworld.gov/ntis/ntisdb.htm) which provides in-depth coverage of scientific, technical and business-related research (the complete database contains more than two million entries) and **NTIS Alert** (http://www.fedworld.gov/ntis/alerts.htm) with customized service in the form of twice-monthly briefings. The URL is scheduled to change to (http://www.ntis.gov).

National Institute of Standards of Technology
http://www.nist.gov

Practitioners of the hard sciences know how important NIST is when making calculations and doing experiments. Learn how to order all of NIST's standard references for chemistry, physics, and other sciences; complete catalogs are available here. Visit any of the laboratories of the National Institute of Standards and Technology. They include the Physics Laboratory, the Chemical Science Laboratory, Computing and Applied Systems or Electronic and Electrical Engineering Laboratories; all are sources of detailed information about research in each field. Don't miss the terrific online exhibit, **A Walk Through Time** (http://physics.nist.gov/GenInt/Time/time.html) to learn about ancient calendars, how watches work and the "atomic" age of time standards.

Four interesting programs at NIST include: the **Advanced Technology Program** (http://www.atp.nist.gov), which since 1990 has been working hand in hand with industry to develop innovative technologies with strong commercial appeal; the **Asia-Pacific Technology Program** (http://www.doc.gov/aptp.html); the **Manufacturing Extension Partnership** (http://www.mep.nist.gov); and the **National Information Infrastructure** (http://nii.nist.gov) which is the home of the so-called "information superhighway" and where you can apply for an NII Award recognizing innovation and excellence in the era of computer and telecommunications networking.

Executive Departments

Time

The Naval Observatory Master Clock
(http://tycho.usno.navy.mil)

A Walk Through Time (National Institute of Standards)
(http://physics.nist.gov/GenInt/Time/time.html)

DEPARTMENT OF DEFENSE
http://www.dtic.dla.mil/defenselink/

DOD is of course responsible for providing the military forces needed to deter war and protect the security of our country. The major elements of these forces are the Army, Navy, Marine Corps, and Air Force; combined, they have about 1.5 million men and women on active duty. They are backed, in case of emergency, by the 1 million members of the reserve components. About 900,000 civilians are employed in DOD.

(The Pentagon, the home of DOD, was built in 1941–1942 on wasteland and swamps astride the Potomac River. The building has 17.5 miles of corridors. Approximately 23,000 employees work there. For Pentagon tour information, call (202) 695–1776.)

The Defenselink home page divides DOD into branches, but hundreds of informative sites that cannot be found under the branch headings. We'll highlight just a few, beginning with elements of the **Defense Technical Information Service** (http://www.dtic.mil):

Bosnia Link
http://www.dtic.mil/bosnia/army

Up-to-the-minute information on the United States presence in Bosnia. Photos and news briefs are updated regularly.

Military Magazines

Airman (Air Force)
(http://www.dtic.dla.mil/airforcelink/pa/airman/cover.htm)

Soldiers (Army)
(http://redstone.army.mil/soldiers/home.html)

Chips (Navy)
(http://www.chips.navy.mil/chips)

Marines
(http://www.usmc.mil/marines/default.htm)

Gulflink

http://www.dtic.dla.mil/gulflink

> Gulflink emerged from the Persian Gulf War and boasts a searchable, declassified document database. A search on anthrax turned up documents on hypothetical biological warfare scenarios as well as specific Middle Eastern locations suspected of housing anthrax.

The Department of Defense Fact File

http://www.dtic.dla.mil/defenselink/factfile

> A comprehensive guide to defense responsibilities, services, command structures, types of armaments, and more. Its primary caveat: "Write it in English, not Pentagonese."

DOD Laboratories

http://www.dtic.dla.mil/labman/projects/list.html

> A gateway to 81 DOD labs, among them the **Aberdeen Test Center** (http://dale.apg.army.mil), **Walter Reed Army Institute of Research** (http://www.wramc .amedd.army.mil), and **Naval Medical Research Institute** (http://www.matmo.army.mil/home.html), which is the online home of the DOD "Telemedicine Test Bed."

National Defense University

http://www.ndu.edu

> The leader in military education, and the home of the **National War College** and the **Institute for National Strategic Studies.** Stop by the **Defense Nexus** library to find a good index of military organizations and information.

National Security Agency

http://www.nsa.gov:8080

> Get a "peek behind the curtain" of the National Security Agency, established in 1952 to be the agent of signals intelligence and communications

Executive Departments

security. An interesting exhibit is the **National Cryptologic Museum** where we learned that, in 1850, an Army doctor named Albert Myer invented a method of communications by line of sight, using signal flags. The Myer flag system was used during the Civil War and became the origin of the Army Signal Corps. Find out about Enigma, used to crack the German messages code in World War II, and peek into the KGB Museum. One of U.S. intelligence's great successes was the VENONA Project—the codename for the effort to collect and decrypt the text of Soviet KGB and GRU messages beginning in the 1940s. Ending a 50 year silence, these documents showing Soviet efforts to infiltrate the highest levels of the U.S. government are now starting to come online.

World War II—"Fifty-Four Years Ago" Archives
http://www.webbuild.com/~jbdavis/ww2.html

WWII vets owe thanks to John Davis (jbdavis@pobox.com), who writes a column "dedicated to keeping the memory of World War II alive" for this private webpage and is constantly compiling first-person accounts, photos, and stories. Send him an e-mail if you are looking for a buddy or have a reunion to announce. Davis frequently updates this archive, which features letters, diaries, documents, speeches, and photo memoirs. Included are first-person accounts of the attack on Pearl Harbor, the Blitz of Malta, the Battle of Guadalcanal, and many other major events.

The Korean War Project
http://www.onramp.net/~hbarker/

A wonderful memorial to the "forgotten war" posted by Hal Baker, the son of a veteran of the 1950–1952 "police action." (Baker is also a cofounder of the Korean War Memorial Trust Fund.)

ACQ Web

http://www.acq.osd.mil

> If you do business with DOD, then be sure to visit the web page of the Office of the Under Secretary of Defense for Acquisition and Technology. Click on the **Office Navigator** to reach the **Acq Web Organizational Chart,** where you'll find the following components:

> Acquisition Reform
>
> Advanced Technology
>
> Atomic Energy
>
> Ballistic Missile Defense
>
> Defense Logistics Agency
>
> Defense Research and Engineering
>
> Economic Security
>
> Environmental Security
>
> Logistics
>
> Operational Test and Evaluation

> The **Ballistic Missile Defense Organization** is the home to the wonderfully named **Office of Strategic Phenomena** (http://vader.nrl.navy.mil/osp.html). And don't miss the **DOD Education Gateway** (http://www.acq.osd.mil/ddre/edugate) where, over the past fifty years, DOD agencies have developed programs in support of science and engineering education supplementing local civilian schools and educating 150,000 dependents in grades K–12. Other aspects of its education program include ROTC scholarships and national defense-related research conducted by graduate students.

Advanced Research Projects Agency

http://www.arpa.mil

> ARPA, DOD's central research and developmental organization, was instrumental in the rise of the Internet.

Executive Departments

Defense Reutilization and Marketing Service
http://www.drms.dla.mil

> In non-DOD speak, this is the home page for U.S. government sales of surplus materials and equipment. There are lots of catalogs and "how to buy" information.

Armylink
http://www.army.mil

> Hundreds of home pages alone can be accessed within Armylink. One of its primary services is to track down personnel and alumni. Many regiments and army organizations have their own pages, and more are being added continuously.

Army Recruiting
http://www.usarec.army.mil

Take a tour of the U.S. Army. Learn about the training programs and educational opportunities, and the Soldier's Creed. If you want more information on the Army, use the online form to have it sent to your home.

Soldiers Magazine
http://www.redstone.army.mil/soldiers/home.html

A monthly online magazine, with stories ranging from current defense issues to profiles of heroes.

LingNet—The Linguist's Network
http://lingnet.army.mil

A fascinating set of links to language-specific information, news and culture.

Command and General Staff College
http://www-cgsc.army.mil

Located at Fort Leavenworth, Kansas, the College educates and trains officers, from captains through generals, at its five schools, including the **Center for Army Leadership. The Combined Arms Research Library** features a large collection of books on military tactics.

U.S. Army War College
http://carlisle-www.army.mil

The Army War College, situated in the Susquehanna Valley of central Pennsylvania, has a number of first-rate online sites, among them: the **Military History Institute,** the **Army Physical Fitness Research Institute** (which features the online book, *Executive Wellness: A Guide for Senior Leaders*), and the **Center for Strategic Leadership.**

Army ROTC
http://www-tradoc.army.mil/rotc/index.html

Everything you need to know about ROTC, from college life to scholarships to a list of participating colleges.

Army Alumni Organizations
http://www.army.mil/vetinfo/vetloc.htm

Hundreds of associations are linked here. A related site is **Army Retirement Services** (http://www.army.mil/retire-p/retire.htm), where you can find out about retirement pay and social security, survivors' benefits plans, preretirement counseling, and back issues of *Army Echoes,* the Army's bulletin for retired soldiers.

U.S. Army Corps of Engineers Information Network
http://www.usace.army.mil

The Army Corps of Engineers manages engineering, construction and real estate programs for the Army, Air Force, and other government agencies.

Fort Benning
http://www.benning.army.mil

Home of the Infantry and the U.S. Army Ranger Training Brigade.

U.S. Military Academy
http://www.usma.edu

Find out all the admissions details, and download the form letters required to get a nomination to West Point. Submit an online form requesting a precandidate questionnaire in preparation for submitting an application. Review profiles of West Point cadets (geographic distribution, SAT and ACT scores, high school activities and honors) and take an online tour of West Point. Sports fans should enjoy the **Go Army!** page. The address is, not surprisingly, (http://www.usma.edu/BeatNavy.html).

Army Research Laboratory
http://info.arl.army. mil

A lab at the forefront of the challenge to marry technology to land warfare. A highlight here is a marvelous history of the computer as told through the historical archive of ENIAC (the first electronic digital computer, developed by Army Ordinance to compute World War II ballistic firing tables), much of which is online (http://ftp.arl.mil /~mike/comphist).

Center for Army Lessons Learned
http://call.army.mil:1100/call.html

"The old saying, 'Live and Learn,' must be reversed in war, for there we 'Learn and Live. . .'"—from a U.S. War Department pamphlet, July 1945. A related site is the **Center of Military History** (http://www .army.mil/cmh-pg/default.htm).

Air Force Link
http://www.dtic.dla.mil/airforcelink/index.html

Your best gateway is **Airforce Sites** (http://www.dtic.mil /airforcelink/sites/), which links to all the major Air Force commands.

Uncle Sam's Academies

Air Traffic Controller Academy
(http://www.ama500.jccbi.gov)

U.S. Air Force Academy
(http://www.usafa.af.mil)

U.S. Coast Guard Academy
(http://www.dot.gov/dotinfo/uscg/hq/uscga/uscga.html)

U.S. Marine Corps University (http://138.156.204.100)

U.S. Merchant Marine Academy
(http://www.usmma.edu)

U.S. Military Academy at West Point
(http://www.usma.edu)

U.S. Naval Academy
(http://www.nadn.navy.mil)

Headquarters U.S. Air Force

http://www.hq.af.mil

Links to the U.S. Air Force Logistics and Personnel home pages.

U.S. Air Force Academy

http://www.usafa.af.mil

Find admissions information, application forms, details about the various majors and training programs, and common questions and answers.

HQ Air Force Personnel Center

http://www.afpc.af.mil

Access to officers' and enlisted personnel's assignments online, plus information affecting Air Force retirees and their families.

Civil Air Patrol

http://www.cap.af.mil

The Civil Air Patrol was created one week before Pearl Harbor, on December 1, 1941. It is the civilian auxiliary to the United States Air Force with more than 1,700 unites and 53,000 members.

Air Combat Command Headquarters

http://www.acc.af.mil

The largest Major Command in the Air Force, with 125,000 active duty/civilian and 110,600 Guard and Reserve personnel, and 21 bases Link here to *Airman* Magazine as well as to a clickable map of the bases (http://www.acc.af.mil/acc_sites.html).

Air Force Reserves

http://www.afres.af.mil

One of the finest Air Force sites online, HQ AFRES features the "Early Bird," a daily compilation of defense-related news distributed by DOD's public affairs office.

U.S. Marine Corps
http://www.hqmc.usmc.mil/

"From the halls of Montezuma to the shores of Tripoli." Read the FAQ's, a history of the Marines and a fact file of all aircraft, vehicles, weapons, and equipment.

Department of the Navy
http://www.navy.mil

The best organized of DOD's major branches, Navy Online is the gateway to all its online resources. A good place to start is the **Navy Public Affairs Library** (http://www.navy.mil/navpalib/.www /welcome.html), where you can get e-mail addresses for those at sea and consult the voluminous fact files for information on aircraft, submarines, and weaponry. From the home page, you can also access the alphabetical listing of the home pages of more than 75 naval sites, from individual ships to the **Naval War College.** A number of carriers now have their own home pages.

The Fleet Numerical Meteorology and Oceanography Center
http://metoc.fnoc.navy.mil

Find out what the waves are going to be like in the Pacific or the Atlantic Ocean by requesting a picture from the Oceanography branch; or request a temperature and precipitation forecast from the meteorology branch; or download visual or infrared satellite images of the United States, provided by a defense satellite.

Planet Earth
http://www.nosc.mil/planet_earth/info.html

This home page is part of the Naval Command, Control and Ocean Surveillance Center, which itself is part of the wonderfully named SPAWAR, or Space and Naval Warfare Systems Command. It's less a site of government information than a magnificent encyclopedia of sites all across the

Executive Departments

World Wide Web. We urge you to visit the Library Floorplan to make use of the vast, categorized subject material.

Naval Observatory

http://www.usno.navy.mil/home.html

What time is it? Timekeeping here is based on an ensemble of cesium beam and hydrogen master atomic clocks. Access the **U.S. Naval Observatory Master Clock** (http://tycho.usno.navy.mil/what.html) to get a precise atomic time measurement.

U.S. Naval Academy

http://www.nadn.navy.mil

Get information about admissions, and the latest Navy sports scores and updates. The **Nimitz Library** is well worth browsing.

Naval Research Laboratory

http://www.nrl.navy.mil

This is the Navy's R&D lab, created in 1923 on the advice of Thomas Edison. An online highlight is the Clementine spacecraft website. Clementine mapped the moon with four cameras over a four-month period in 1994. Its mission (part of the Deep Space Program Science Experiment) is to use the moon to demonstrate lightweight components and sensor performance. There are truly sensational graphic images of earth and the moon, with links to additional images at the Clementine site at the U.S. Geological Survey. For scores of other noteworthy sites, consult NRL's Alphabetical Index. One must-see is the **Space Science Division** (http://bradbury.nrl.navy.mil/general/ssd.html).

Naval Undersea Warfare Center

http://www.nuwc.navy.mil

A full-spectrum R&D and fleet support center for submarines and undersea weapons systems. Learn about torpedoes, periscopes, tactical unmanned underwater vehicles (UUVs), and undersea warfare.

DEPARTMENT OF EDUCATION
http://www.ed.gov

The Education Department establishes policy, administers resources, and coordinates most federal assistance to education at all levels. Along with the Commerce and Health and Human Services departments, this is one of the most useful sites within the executive branch. Its many publications, interactive sites, and links will be appreciated by students, teachers, and administrators.

A Teacher's Guide to the Department of Education
http://www.ed.gov/pubs/TeachersGuide

An excellent hypertext version of the latest edition of the standard Education Department Guide. Find out about current Education Department initiatives, grant programs, services and resources. At the **Office of Educational Research and Improvement** (http://www.ed.gov/pubs/TeachersGuide/pt15.html) you'll learn about 24 research and development centers, such as the **National Center on Adult Literacy** at the University of Pennsylvania (http://litserver.literacy.upenn.edu) and the **National Research Center on Student Learning** at the University of Pittsburgh (http://www.lrdc.pitt.edu). Teachers will find another fine program sponsored by the Education Department at the **Eisenhower National Clearinghouse for Mathematics and Science Education** (http://www.enc.org). One of the highlights at the Eisenhower center is "The Digital Dozen," which features a monthly listing of outstanding math and science Internet sites.

Executive Departments

A Researcher's Guide to the Department of Education
http://www.ed.gov/pubs/ResearchersGuide

A guide to funding within the Education Department. A related site is **Applying for Grants** (http://www.ed.gov/pubs/KnowAbtGrants). Anyone can apply for funds to run an educational studies program. The online guide is designed to take the fear out of the process. There are specific details about the types of grants and programs, and the application process. A complete list of available grants is posted at (gopher://gopher.ed.gov/11/gen_progs/guide).

Publications for Parents
http://www.ed.gov/pubs/parents.html

The Education Department is a source for thousands of documents, brochures, and other publications for parents, teachers, and administrators. Available at this site is the "Helping Your Child Series," twelve hypertext pamphlets specifically aimed at parents. The titles are:

Helping Your Child Learn Math
Helping Your Child Learn Geography
Helping Your Child Learn Responsible Behavior
Helping Your Child Learn Science
Helping Your Child Learn History
Helping Your Child with Homework
Helping Your Child Get Ready for School
Helping Your Child Succeed in School
Helping Your Child Improve in Test Taking
Helping Your Child Learn to Read
Helping Your Child Learn to Write Well
Helping Your Child Use the Library

This fine series includes experiments that parents can do with their children: in science, for example, an activity exploring photosynthesis; in reading, a list of tips on how best to read to a newborn baby. A related document, **Preparing Your Child for College** (http://www.ed.gov/pubs/Prepare), discusses types of colleges, how to choose, financing, and links to other useful resources.

ERIC: Educational Resources Information Center
http://www.aspensys.com/eric

ERIC is the largest education database in the world. It contains more than 850,000 records of teaching and curricula guides, books, journal articles, and research reports—a national information system designed to provide users with ready access to this trove of materials. Established in 1966, ERIC was, according to the Education Department, the first commercial online database.

ERIC is at the forefront of efforts to make education information available through computer networks; the database is offered in many formats at hundreds of locations. Your primary access points for collecting, abstracting, and indexing materials for the ERIC database are the **16 Clearinghouses,** situated at universities. We list them here by subject of specialty:

Adult, Career and Vocational Education
http://www.acs.ohio-state.edu/units/education/cete/ericacve/index.html

Assessment and Evaluation
http://www.cua.edu/www/eric_ae

Community Colleges
http://www.gse.ucla.edu/ERIC/eric.html

Counseling and Student Services
http://www.uncg.edu:80/~ericcas2

Disabilities and Gifted Education
gopher://ericir.syr.edu:70/11/Clearinghouses/16houses/ERIC_EC

Educational Management
http://darkwing.uoregon.edu/~ericcem/home.html

Elementary and Early Childhood Education
http://ericps.ed.uiuc.edu/ericeece.html

National Parent Information Network
http://ericps.ed.uiuc.edu/npin/npinhome.html

Information and Technology
gopher://ericir.syr.edu:70/11/Clearinghouses/16houses/CIT

Languages and Linguistics
http://ericir.syr.edu/ericll

Reading, English and Communication
http://www.indiana.edu/~eric_rec

Rural Education and Small Schools
http://www.ael.org/~eric/eric.html

Science, Mathematics, and Environmental Education
http://www.ericse.ohio-state.edu

Social Studies/Social Science Education
http://www.indiana.edu/~ssdc/eric-chess.html

Teaching and Teacher Education
http://www.ericsp.org

Urban Education
http://eric-web.tc.columbia.edu

Best Teacher Sites

The Digital Classroom
(http://www.nara.gov/nara/digital/classroom.html)

Electronic Smithsonian
(http://www.si.edu/electrsi/start.htm)

AskERIC (Educational Resources Information Center)
(http://ericir.syr.edu)

GLOBE Program (Global Learning and Observations to Benefit
the Environment)
(http://www.globe.gov)

JASON Project (http://seawifs.gsfc.nasa.gov/scripts/JASON.html)

Learning About the Holocaust
(http://www.ushmm.org/holo.htm)

Learning Web
(http://www.usgs.gov/education/index.html)

National Center for Education Statistics
(http://www.ed.gov/NCES)

NASA Spacelink
(http://spacelink.msfc.nasa.gov)

A Teacher's Guide to the Department of Education
(http://www.ed.gov/pubs/TeachersGuide)

White House for Kids
(http://www.whitehouse.gov/WH/kids/html/kidshome.html)

The Whole Frog Project
(http://www-itg.lbl.gov/ITG.hm.pg.docs/Whole.Frog/Whole.Frog.html)

For a one-page directory of these Clearinghouses (and adjunct Clearing-houses), go to (http://aspensys3.aspensys.com/eric/barak.html). Note: These are likely some of the most useful educational sites you'll find anywhere on the Internet.

The ERIC Document Reproduction Service produces and sells microfiche and hard copies of documents in the ERIC database. For further information, go to (http://edrs.com).

Hats off to a remarkable program called the **AskERIC Virtual Library** (http://ericir.syr.edu). In a partnership linking Syracuse University, the Department of Education, and Sun Computers, this Virtual Library features ERIC lesson plans for teachers, the Search ERIC Database (covering records between 1991 and 1995), Ask ERIC Info Guides, and a Q&A service to communicate with other professionals at all levels of schooling.

If you have questions that cannot be answered online, call (800) LET-ERIC or send e-mail to acceric@inst.ed.gov.

The Student Guide: Financial Aid from the U. S. Department of Education
http://www.ed.gov/prog_info/SFA/StudentGuide

The Department of Education is trying to make financial aid easier to understand by putting the entire Student Guide to Financial Aid online, including details about types of aid, the borrower's responsibilities and rights, and deferment and loan information. Click on **FAFSA Express** (http://www.ed.gov/offices/OPE/express.html) and you can file a paperless financial aid application. Use either a toll-free number or an e-mail address for customer service in filing your application. FAFSA, which is an acronym for Free Application for Federal Student Aid, is one of many highlights of the **Office of Post-Secondary Education** (http://www.ed.gov/offices/OPE).

National Institute for Literacy
http://novel.nifl.gov

> Join in the several online forums discussing literacy issues, learn about grants for literacy work, or read over the Institute's newsletter. Search for documents or programs using keywords; use the listings to find literacy and resource centers; find out about recent legislation affecting literacy funding and grants; link into other useful Internet resources. See the **Literacy Directory Home Page** (http://novel.nifl.gov/litdir /index.html), a large and comprehensive listing of Internet sites that have literacy and adult education information.

Catalogue of Federal Domestic Assistance
http://www.ed.gov/programs.html#CFDA

> A complete list of every agency and department in the government that provides money to grant-making entities.

Programs and Services
http://www.ed.gov/programs.html

> This site shows the range of current Education Department programs, beginning with the text of the famous 1983 report, "A Nation at Risk." Scroll down to the bottom of this page to find a clickable map of **Educational Resources by State.** This is an especially useful tool because many of the department's programs are administered at the local level.

National Network of Regional Educational Laboratories
http://www.nwrel.org/national/regional-labs.html

> Ten regional labs supported by contracts with the Department are planning the R&D of education in the future. This clickable map takes you to the ten districts and gives you contact names, phone numbers, and addresses.

Executive Departments

ED Supported Sites
http://www.ed.gov/EdRes/EdFed/OtherED.html

A gateway to many organizations supported by the Education Department, including:

National Early Childhood Technical Assistance System
http://www.nectas.unc.edu

Supports policies and programs for young children with disabilities and for their families.

The National Rehabilitation Information Center
http://www.naric.com/naric/home.html

Disseminates information on spinal cord and head injuries, the Americans with Disabilities Act, and vocational rehabilitation.

Regional Resource and Federal Centers
http://www.aed.org/special.ed/rrfc1.html

Special education services to state education agencies in the fifty states.

National Clearinghouse for Bilingual Education
http://www.ncbe.gwu.edu

National Center for Research in Vocational Education
http://vocserve.berkeley.edu

School-to-Work Gateway
http://www.stw.ed.gov

The School-to-Work Opportunities Act of 1994 provides seed money to public and private partnerships at the local level to train today's students for tomorrow's high-skilled careers. Use the clickable map at (http://www.stw.ed.gov/grants/grants.htm) to find out about grant opportunities available.

Best Sites for College, Grad, and Postgrad Students

America's Job Bank
(http://www.ajb.dni.us)

Career Planning Center (National Academy of Sciences)
(http://www2.nas.edu/cpc/index.html)

Federal Job Announcement Search
(http://www.fedworld.gov/jobs/jobsearch.html)

National Science Foundation
(http://www.nsf.gov)

Naval Research Laboratory Library
(http://infonext.nrl.navy.mil/job.html)

Occupational Information Network (ONET)
(http://www.doleta.gov/programs/onet/onet_hp.htm)

Occupational Outlook Handbook
(http://stats.bls.gov/ocohome.htm)

School-to-Work Gateway
(http://www.stw.ed.gov)

An unofficial government service called FEDIX, or the Federal Information Exchange (http://web.fie.com) is an extremely useful information retrieval service that links government and higher education. FEDIX can help colleges and research organizations locate funding and grant opportunities, contact key government personnel, secure free computer and research equipment, and discover minority opportunities.

DEPARTMENT OF ENERGY

http://www.doe.gov

The mission of the Department of Energy is to provide the technical information and scientific foundation for efficiency in energy use. A good place to begin is at **Information Services** accessible from the homepage where you'll find the program offices of DOE, among them the **Office of Fusion Energy,** the **Office of Civilian Radioactive Management,** and the **Office of Environmental Management,** all of which have sophisticated websites. Science educators and academics should particularly note and pay close attention to the many laboratory sites affiliated with DOE, which lead our entries.

U.S. Department of Energy Server Map

http://www.doe.gov/html/doe/infolink/usdoemap.html

A clickable map of the country, highlighting the twenty-one laboratories affiliated with or run by DOE, which carry on cutting-edge research. Among them are:

Lawrence Livermore National Laboratory
http://www.llnl.gov

Operated by the University of California under a contract with DOE. Located at the Laboratory is the **National Energy Research Supercomputer Center** (http://www.nersc.gov), the principal supplier of high-performance computing and networking services to the nationwide energy research community.

Stanford Linear Accelerator Center
http://www.slac.stanford.edu

A basic research lab probing the structure of matter at the atomic scale with X rays and at even smaller scales with electron and positron beams. The lab is operated by Stanford University, under a contract with DOE.

National Renewable Energy Laboratory
http://info.nrel.gov

> The nation's leading lab for renewable energy and energy efficiency research. Research areas include wind technology and photovoltaics.

The Superconducting Super Collider Project
http://www.ssc.gov

> RIP: The project was DOE-supported, but in 1993 the House of Representatives halted the project after fourteen miles of tunneling were completed and $2 billion were spent. The lab is in final shutdown phase, but its archives are still online.

Fermi National Accelerator Laboratory
http://www.fnal.gov

> Home of the world's most powerful particle accelerator.

Ernest Orlando Lawrence Berkeley National Laboratory
http://www.lbl.gov

> Ernest Orland Lawrence, inventor of the cyclotron, founded this mecca of particle physics and biosciences in 1931.

Oak Ridge National Laboratory
http://www.ornl.gov

> A wide range of basic and applied research and development to advance the nation's energy resources, environmental quality, and economic competitiveness.

Brookhaven National Laboratory
http://suntid.bnl.gov:8080/bnl.html

> Interdisciplinary programs seek to gain a deeper understanding of the laws of nature.

Executive Departments

Argonne National Laboratory

http://www.anl.gov

> One of the first and largest energy research centers, Argonne is now constructing the Advanced Photon Source, which will provide the most brilliant X-ray beams for research in materials science.

Los Alamos National Laboratory

http://www.lanl.gov

> First known as Project Y, Los Alamos was established in 1943 as part of the Manhattan Engineering District to develop the world's first atomic bomb under the leadership of J. Robert Oppenheimer. Located on 433 square miles of mesas and canyons north of Santa Fe, New Mexico, Los Alamos has a multidisciplinary program ranging from national security to molecular biology.

Office of Defense Programs

http://www.dp.doe.gov

> Ensures the safety, reliability, and performance of nuclear weapons without underground nuclear testing. Be sure to visit the site for **The Trinity Test** (http://www2.dp.doe.gov/MapServe/text/TRINITY.HTM), which relives the first nuclear blast, on July 16, 1945, in New Mexico. Look at photos, read historical documents, and become a virtual participant of the fiftieth anniversary symposium.

Energy Efficiency and Renewable Energy Network

http://www.eren.doe.gov

> An archive of energy-related pictures, solar radiation maps, and more. The Network's **Clearinghouse** (http://www.nrel.gov /documents/erec_fact_sheets/erec.html) has online books and brochures with energy-saving tips, including "Energy Saving Tips

for Small Businesses," "Heat Pumps," "Selecting a New Hot Water Heater." Free printed copies of these brochures can be ordered through forms online.

Alternative Fuels Data Center
http://www.afdc.doe.gov

Access maps of refueling locations, find out how your city is involved in the Clean Cities partnership, and consult the Fuel Economy Guide for estimates of miles per gallon for the vehicles of the future.

Energy Information Administration
http://www.eia.doe.gov

A mountain of data regarding different forms of energy—natural gas, coal, petroleum, electricity, and renewable energy sources. For forecasts of consumption and production, go to the **EIA Analyses and Forecasts.** At the **Energy Information Highway,** download The International Energy Database and Country Analyses Briefs, which produces detailed, regularly updated information about most of the major energy-producing and energy-consuming countries and regions (such as North Sea, Panama Canal, and Persian Gulf). Maps, political background, and historical information are included. Also, find out how to obtain a trial copy of the EIA CD-ROM, which will regularly offer new statistics, documents, and publications.

Office of Human Radiation Experiments
http://www.ohre.doe.gov

In 1994, it was officially revealed that, during the Cold War, the U.S. government performed radiation experiments on humans. View the recently declassified documents, find out more information about the content and location of document stashes (describing the experiments and people involved; some may still be classified), see photographs from the experiments, and search the database for more information. The FAQ list is extremely helpful for anyone who may have been involved in one of these experiments. Guidelines cover how to obtain one's records, confidentiality, compensation, medical concerns, and more.

The U.S. Department of Energy Business Page

http://www.pr.doe.gov/prbus.html

A complete guide to contracts, bids, and performance and payment requirements, plus information about current programs that are soliciting bids, what the department buys, opportunities for small business, links to regional/local procurement office home pages, and other important info. Documents include "Guide for the Submission of Unsolicited Proposals" and "General Information on Contracting with the Federal Government."

Open Net

http://www.doe.gov/html/osti/opennet/openscr.html

Early in 1996, DOE released for the first time an accounting of U.S. plutonium production and use. This was one of 2 million pages of documents that have been declassified since 1993. Open Net, with its searchable database, will be the home for these documents (some are "declassified," others are "sanitized" or "redacted").

Office of Science Education Programs

http://www.doe.gov/html/ouse/ousehome.html

This office spearheads DOE's role in improving science, engineering, and technical education. Two terrific interactive science education projects were developed by the Lawrence Berkeley and Lawrence Livermore laboratories:

The Whole Frog Project
http://www-itg.lbl.gov/ITG.hm.pg.docs/Whole.Frog /Whole.Frog.html

> Dissect a virtual frog and learn the basic concepts of both anatomy and computer-based 3D visualization. The goal of the Whole Frog Project is to educate high school biology students. (Some technical data and skills are required.) This is the first in a series of attempts to teach anatomy without having to kill and dissect living creatures. Not a toy; really useful for teachers.

Hobbyists' Heavens

Earth Science Information Center at USGS (Maps)
(http://www-nmd.usgs.gov/esic/esic.html)

National Postal Museum
(http://www.si.edu/organiza/museums/postal/start.htm)

North American Breeding Bird Survey
(http://www.mbr.nbs.gov/bbs/bbs.html)

PLANTS Database at U.S. Department of Agriculture
(http://plants.usda.gov:80/plants)

Stamp Archives at United States Postal Service
(http://www.usps.gov/postofc/stamps.htm)

U.S. Mint (Coins)
(http://www.usmint.gov)

Executive Departments

Microworlds

http://www.lbl.gov/MicroWorlds

> What are polymers and why are they so useful? How do scientists make machines that can fit through the eye of a needle? Aimed at grades 9–12, these are the kinds of questions that Microworlds, subtitled "Exploring the Structure of Materials Science Education," tries to answer. To explore the atom in greater detail, go to **The Particle Adventure** (http://pdg.lbl.gov/cpep/adventure.html).

Department of Energy 1-800 Information Lines

http://www.hr.doe.gov/800numb.html

> A directory of fifteen DOE 1-800 numbers, including numbers where the public can order DOE brochures and documents, and safety and whistleblower hotlines.

Council on Environmental Quality

http://ceq.eh.doe.gov

> Created by the National Environmental Policy Act (NEPA) of 1969, the CEQ recommends environmental policy to the President and analyzes trends in the national environment. From the home page, click on **NEPA Net** to search DOE's environmental impact and environmental assessment statements. And be sure to visit the **Environmental Sites/Data Links** where you'll find a stunning map of the United States followed by a set of topical links to Endangered Species, Pollution Prevention, Wetlands, and other public and private sites.

DEPARTMENT OF HEALTH AND HUMAN SERVICES
http://www.os.dhhs.gov

Health and Human Services is the government department that is most intimately involved with the nation's human concerns, from newborn infants to our most elderly citizens. A remarkable array of services is available through its web pages, most notably those of the Public Health Service, which oversees the Centers for Disease Control and the National Institutes of Health. The Social Security Administration, once under the domain of HHS, became an independent agency on March 31, 1995 (see the listing under Independent Agencies). At the **Office of the Assistant Secretary for Planning and Evaluation** (http://aspe.os.dhhs.gov) you'll find the latest policy information on welfare reform, disability, aging and long-term care, children and youth, and health care reform. Particularly useful is the Green Book Overview of Entitlement Programs—descriptions and historical data about Social Security, unemployment compensation, Aid for Dependent Children (AFDC), and welfare.

Administration for Children and Families
http://www.acf.dhhs.gov

An excellent source of vital information that brings together a broad range of federal programs, including: Aid to Families with Dependent Children, At-Risk Child Care, Child Welfare Services, Community Services Block Grant, Foster Care and Adoption Assistance, Head Start, and the National Center on Child Abuse and Neglect.

Administration on Aging
http://www.aoa.dhhs.gov/aoa/index.html

Information on the elderly includes statistical profiles of America's older population and useful fact sheets on elder care such as "Looking Out for

Executive Departments

Depression," "Vaccinations Aren't Just Kid Stuff," and "Decisions about Retirement Living." **The Age Pages** (http://www.aoa.dhhs.gov/aoa/pages/info.html/#agepage) have a selection of health brochures on topics such as AIDS, sex, flu, prostate problems, health quackery, and "Life Extension: Science or Science-Fiction?" **The Eldercare Locator** (http://www.aoa.dhhs.gov/aoa/pages /loctrnew.html) is a service dedicated to helping elderly persons and their caregivers find local support resources. Call 1-800-677-1116 or visit here for more information. Included are e-mail addresses of services, discussion groups, and other referral sources.

The National Health Information Center
http://nhic-nt.health.org

Uncle Sam's health information referral service for matching consumers with health professionals and organizations. Click on the **Toll-Free Number** page and you'll have the (800) numbers for an alphabet soup of more than 400 organizations within and outside of government. Also useful is the **Federal Health Information Centers and Clearinghouses,** an incredibly valuable service that distributes literature, provides referrals, and answers inquiries.

Office of Minority Health
http://www.os.dhhs.gov/progorg/ophs/omh

Be sure to visit the **Resource Center** to learn about minority health programs, databases, and funding sources. Click on regional and state contacts for names, addresses, and phone numbers of health professionals around the country.

Centers for Disease Control
http://www.cdc.gov

Vital for anyone who needs research data. Many of the best resources can be found through one of the eleven centers, institutes, and offices. Here are a few:

National Institute for Occupational Safety and Health
http://www.cdc.gov/niosh/homepage.html

Documents about diagnosing and preventing everything from carpal tunnel syndrome to homicide in the workplace. Publications, like "Pocket Guide to Chemical Hazards," are available.

National Center for Health Statistics
http://www.cdc.gov/nchswww/nchshome.htm

Access authoritative data on birth, death, divorce, and marriage statistics. The Center has numerous publications and electronic data products; many may be requested using an online form. **Where to Write for Vital Records** (http://www.cdc.gov/nchswww/w2w-all.htm) is a handy reference when you need a certified copy of a birth certificate, marriage license, or divorce decree. An official record of each certificate is filed according to the locality where the event occurred. This publication contains info necessary to obtain copies of records from the vital statistics offices of all fifty states and the U.S. territories.

National Center for Infectious Diseases
http://www.cdc.gov/ncidod/ncid.htm

Learn about new, reemerging, and drug-resistant infections, and read current and back issues of the professional journal, *Emerging Infectious Diseases,* now online. A related and extremely useful site **Selected Prevention and Control Areas** (http://www.cdc.gov/ncidod/diseases/diseases.htm)

Executive Departments

links to more than twenty diseases, among them: Epstein-Barr, gonorrhea, Lyme disease, malaria, and rabies.

National Center for Environmental Health
http://www.cdc.gov/nceh/i:/cehweb/nceh/Oncehhom.htm

Brochures and fact sheets on lead poisoning, carbon monoxide poisoning, and fetal alcohol syndrome. Its divisions include Birth Defects and Developmental Disabilities.

National Center for Chronic Disease Prevention
http://www.cdc.gov/nccdphp/nccdhome.htm

Programs include Surveillance, Modifying Risk Factors (tobacco, nutrition), Disease Prevention (diabetes, breast and cervical cancer, cardiovascular disease), and Maternal and Infant Health.

National Center for HIV, Sexually Transmitted Diseases, and Tuberculosis
http://www.cdc.gov/nchstp/od/nchstp.html

This center (NCHSTP) is your gateway to home pages for each of these conditions. At **HIV/AIDS Prevention** (http://www.cdc.gov/nchstp/hiv_aids/dhap.htm), you'll find a state-of-the-art web server for vital information and statistics. Three other crucial, related sites can be referenced here: **National AIDS Clearinghouse** (http://www.cdcnac .org), which offers truly comprehensive information for people working in the fields of HIV prevention, care and support, and daily AIDS summaries from sources such as the *American Medical News, AIDS Treatment News,* the *Advocate* and the *Journal of the AMA;* **AIDS Clinical Trials Information Service** (http://www.actis.org) where you'll find a national database for evaluating and understanding HIV; and, at the National Library of Medicine, the **Health Services/Technology Assessment Text** (http://text.nlm .nih.gov) where you can submit a data request from the HIV/AIDS Treatment Information Service and find English and Spanish language versions of guidelines for understanding and managing HIV.

There are a number of other exceptional websites within CDC, among them:

Travel Information
http://www.cdc.gov/travel/travel.html

> A clickable map calls up information about health problems and their prevention in every region of the world. Learn, for example, about general food and water guidelines (to prevent diarrhea); the "Blue Sheet," which lists countries with cholera, yellow fever, and plague; vaccine suggestions and requirements; and the "Green Sheet," which evaluates all the cruise ships that sail into and out of American ports.

CDC Prevention Guidelines Database
http://wonder.cdc.gov/wonder/prevguid/prevguid.htm

> A compendium of all official guidelines and recommendations published by the CDC for the prevention of diseases, injuries, and disabilities.

Morbidity and Mortality Weekly Report
http://www.cdc.gov/epo/mmwr/mmwr.html

> Another professional journal that's now online. You can electronically subscribe to the mailing list for future issues and announcements. The material is based on weekly reports to CDC by State Health Departments accessible through (http://www.cdc.gov/epo/mmwr/medassn.html).

CDC WONDER
http://wonder.cdc.gov

> A single point for access to many CDC reports, guidelines, and data. The Search and Query function will tell you how to get an ID account to use the service.

Executive Departments

Food and Drug Administration
http://www.fda.gov

It is the job of the FDA to make sure that our foods, medicines, and medical devices are safe and effective. The home page, headlined "Welcome to Internet FDA," gives you immediate access to ten topic areas, from animal drugs to biologics, cosmetics, human drugs, and foods and toxicology. At the **Center for Food Safety** (http://vm.cfsan.fda.gov/list.html), find out about food additives, pesticides, protecting children from iron poisoning, foodborne illness (*E. coli*), food and drug interactions, and the risk in eating raw oysters, among other subjects. Go to **Food Labeling** (http://vm.cfsan.fda .gov/label.html) to learn about the food pyramid and the newest edition of *Dietary Guidelines for Americans*. One of the most useful gopher sites is the **Center for Drug Evaluation and Research** (gopher:// gopher.cder.fda.gov), which regulates prescription and over-the-counter medicines. Find out what drugs have been approved. Vets and animal lovers will want to visit the **Center for Veterinary Medicine** (http:// www.cvm.fda.gov).

National Institutes of Health
http://www.nih.gov/home.html

One of the world's foremost centers for medical research. Click on **Institutes and Offices** and you'll have access to any of its twenty-four separate institutes, centers, and divisions. Because these divisions are of such immediate concern to professionals and laypeople alike, we've itemized the addresses for the major institutes here:

National Cancer Institute
http://www.nci.nih.gov

National Center for Human Genome Research
http://www.nchgr.nih.gov

National Center for Research Resources
http://www.ncrr.nih.gov

National Eye Institute
http://www.nei.nih.gov

National Heart, Lung and Blood Institute
http://www.nhlbi.nih.gov/nhlbi/nhlbi.html

National Institute on Alcohol Abuse and Alcoholism
http://www.niaaa.nih.gov

National Institute of Allergy and Infectious Diseases
http://www.niaid.nih.gov

National Institute of Arthritis and Musculoskeletal and Skin Diseases
http://www.nih.gov/niams

National Institute of Child Health and Human Development
http://www.nih.gov/nichd

National Institute of Diabetes and Digestive and Kidney Diseases
http://www.niddk.nih.gov

National Institute of Dental Research
http://www.nidr.nih.gov

National Institute on Drug Abuse
http://www.nida.nih.gov

National Institute of General Medical Sciences
http://www.nih.gov/nigms

National Institute of Mental Health
http://www.nimh.nih.gov

Executive Departments

National Institute of Neurological Disorders and Stroke
http://www.nih.gov/ninds

National Institute of Nursing Research
http://www.nih.gov/ninr

To give you an idea of the range of information and materials you'll find here, let's take a closer look at the **National Cancer Institute.** Click on the **International Cancer Information Center** (http://wwwicic .nci.nih.gov), and you'll find CancerNet, a searchable bibliography with treatment summaries for both patients and health professionals. Click on the **Division of Clinical Sciences** and you'll learn how patients and their physicians can explore experimental treatment right at the NIH Clinical Center. **Kid's Home,** a marvelous source of information for children undergoing treatment, features online pictures, stories, and poems for and by children, and guides for parents such as "Talking to Your Child about Cancer."

Another example is the range of publications at the **National Institute for Mental Health** where you can get truly expert information on a dozen specific topics: Anxiety Disorders, Depression, Eating Disorders, Learning Disabilities, Panic Disorder, and Schizophrenia. Under Attention Deficit Hyperactivity Disorder, you'll find such concrete advice as "Coping Strategies for Teens and Adults with ADHD," and "Facts and Myths About Medication and Self-Esteem."

A final example is AIDS-related information that can be accessed via a gopher at the **National Institute of Allergy and Infectious Diseases** (gopher://gopher.niaid.nih.gov:70/11/aids), which, together with CDC's National AIDS Clearinghouse (cited above), constitute perhaps the most comprehensive pair of sources of information on AIDS anywhere.

Consult each institute or center for this kind of in-depth information.

One other part of the NIH deserves special attention: **National Library of Medicine** (http://www.nlm.nih.gov), the world's largest medical library (over 5 million medical books and journals), often called the "Fort Knox of health information." The Library has several databases accessible from here including MEDLARS, a computerized system of databases pertinent to biomedical research and patient care, and MEDLINE, one of the best known and most heavily used biomedical bibliographic databases. Many of these databases require registration and a password; information on how to obtain these is listed on the site.

The Library coordinates the activities of the **National Network of Libraries of Medicine** (http://www.nnlm.nlm.nih.gov), where you can find a clickable map to take you to one of eight regional medical libraries.

At the **National Center for Biotechnology Information** (http://www.ncbi.nlm.nih.gov), you'll find Gen Bank, the NIH genetic sequence database that collects all known DNA sequences from scientists around the world.

Medical researchers and scholars will find superb online exhibits including **Here Today, Here Tomorrow: Varieties of Medical Ephemera** (http://www.nlm.nih.gov/exhibition/ephemera/ephemara .html) and **On-Line Images from the History of Medicine,** (http://wwwoli.nlm.nih.gov/databases/olihmd/olihmd.html) a trip through four centuries of medical knowledge featuring over 60,000 images.

Premed students and others may want to visit **The Visible Human Project** (http://www.nlm.nih.gov/research/visible/visible_human .html), a complete anatomically detailed, three-dimensional representation of the male and female human body. To actually see and use the data, you must subscribe to the service, but you can view sample images.

Executive Departments

Department of Housing and Urban Development

http://www.hud.gov

> HUD offers a great deal of information for potential home buyers. If you're in the market for a house, you can compute current mortgage plans using online calculation systems, and preview the housing conditions in most regions of the country through links to HUD's eighty local offices. Most HUD programs are operated through intermediaries (e.g., cities, nonprofit groups, mortgage bankers, and housing authorities), which is why the clickable table that leads to the field office closest to you (http://www.hud.gov/local.html) is so useful.

Community Center

http://www.hud.gov/communit.html

> The information center for HUD's Office of Community Planning is your entry point to programs that can spur growth and create new opportunities in your neighborhood. Featured is "Step-Up," billed as "a job training program for low-income people that works," and a discussion of empowerment zones and enterprise communities.

CodeTalk for Native Americans

http://www.codetalk.fed.us

> Learn about the valorous history of the Choctaw and Navajo code talkers during World Wars I and II in this interesting home page that is billed as "The Information SuperHighway Running Through Indian Country." Click on **Topics of Interest** and you'll find scores of government information sources on education, health, natural resources, and gaming that are of special interest to Native Americans. Join various online forums to discuss current issues, download documents, and get a calendar of events, a list of Internet resources, and other contacts.

Buying a Home
http://www.hud.gov/buying.html

> For first-time buyers, publications include "Guide to Single-Family Home Mortgage Insurance," "Home Buyers' Vocabulary," explanations of the mortgage application process, closing costs, and so on.

Marketplace
http://www.hud.gov/business.html

> Here, find out how you get the latest information on mortgage loans and HUD properties for sale, including a weekly listing of multifamily homes.

EZ/EC—The Empowerment Zone and Enterprise Community Program
http://www.ezec.gov

> The motto for the EZ/EC program is "Building Communities Together." Go to **EZ/EC Communities** on the home page for a clickable map of the United States to access state programs. In one part of the **Community Toolbox** (http://www.ezec.gov/toolbox/guide/et/et.html), learn about the Jacob K. Javits Gifted and Talented Students Education Program, Title IV (the Bilingual Education Act) grant competitions, and other programs designed to provide job training for youths with disabilities.

Executive Departments

DEPARTMENT OF THE INTERIOR
http://www.doi.gov

As the nation's principal conservation agency, Interior has the responsibility for most of Uncle Sam's nationally owned public lands and natural resources. The Forest Service is housed at the Department of Agriculture, but most of the other treasures of America's Great Outdoors are administered here—including the National Park Service, the U.S. Fish and Wildlife Service, and the Bureau of Land Management. Another division of Interior is the U.S. Geological Survey, the government's official mapmaker. Natural resources mean cultural resources, and one of the wonders of Interior is the range of national monuments it oversees, including the Civil War battlefields. Historians as well as travelers and outdoorspeople will relish the many great sites here.

Bureau of Land Management
http://www.blm.gov

The Bureau of Land Management administers more than 270 million acres of America's great outdoors—about one-eighth of the nation—most of which are located in 11 Western states, including Alaska. Its domain includes 90 million acres of forested lands, 25 wilderness areas in eight states, livestock grazing, wild horse and burro adoptions, and minerals programs. Use the clickable national map to access state and regional offices.

U.S. Fish and Wildlife Service
http://www.fws.gov

From migratory birds to endangered species, FWS conserves and protects wildlife refuges, waterfowl protection areas, and fish hatcheries, through the National Wildlife Refuge System. The System began in

1903 when President Theodore Roosevelt designated three-acre Pelican Island in Florida as a bird sanctuary. Today, 500 refuges encompass more than 91 million acres of habitats. Here are the highlights of the Fish and Wildlife Service:

The National Wildlife Refuge System

http://bluegoose.arw.r9.fws.gov/

> Stunning visual images are ubiquitous at this site. Go to the Index and call up the **Refuge System Brochure** for an introduction to individual refugees, organized alphabetically by state or by refuge unit.

Endangered Species Program

http://www.fws.gov/~r9endspp/endspp.html

> Read the *Endangered Species Bulletin* and use a clickable map at (http://www.fws.gov/~r9endspp/stat-reg.html) to find state-by-state authoritative information on all endangered species of plants and animals under FWS jurisdiction. One especially informative site, **Box Score** (http://www.fws.gov/~r9endspp/boxscore.html), shows a total of 753 endangered species (320 animals, 433 plants) and 206 that are threatened (114 animals, 92 plants), broken out by group (mammals, birds, reptiles, crustaceans, insects, and so on).

Coastal Ecosystems

http://www.fws.gov/~cep/cepcode.html

> Online maps, graphs, and photos highlight the Delaware Bay, the Gulf of Maine, and southern New England.

National Wetlands Inventory

http://www.nwi.fws.gov

> A browseable list of plant species found in wetlands and a searchable database of wetlands citations.

Executive Departments

Park Net—National Park Service

http://www.nps.gov

The National Park Service is dedicated to conserving unimpaired the natural and cultural resources of the nation's parklands. This best-known bureau at Interior is also one of the most notable sites in Uncle Sam's web. You can plan a visit to any of the 365 different units in the National Park System, which covers more than 80 million acres in forty-nine states and territories, and includes national parks, monuments, battlefields, historic sites, seashores, scenic rivers, trails, and the White House. The NPS maintains close to 30,000 campsites in 440 campgrounds; reservations are available at thirteen of the parks.

The Electronic Visitor Center (http://www.nps.gov/facts .html) gives entrance and camping fees, how to prepare for a park visit, frequently asked questions (what are the biggest/smallest /most visited parks?), volunteer information, and a downloadable statistical abstract of the NPS.

Visit Your National Parks (http://www.nps.gov/parks.html) lets you search for parks by name, state, region, or theme. Basic information on each park site includes addresses and phone numbers to contact for more information. Some of the larger parks have pictures and links to their own home pages with maps and hiking and camping guides. Spend some time at Yosemite or the Grand Canyon and you'll be tempted to click your way through a dozen more sites. Newly added are the Washington Monument and Antietam Battlefield, so it's worth checking in often.

Links to the Past (http://www.cr.nps.gov) offers a number of remarkable historical resources from the National Park Service, among them:

National Register of Historic Places

http://www.cr.nps.gov/nr/home.html

America's official list of historic properties worthy of preservation. The register consists of 65,000 properties, searchable by state or territory. Learn how historic places are identified, turned into landmarks, and preserved.

Lighthouses and Ships Within the National Park System
http://www.cr.nps.gov/history/maritime/maripark.html

> An inventory of scores of historic lighthouses and ships
> with pictures, architectural details, and visitor information.

Civil War Battlefields
http://www.cr.nps.gov/abpp/battles/Contents.html

> Read the report of the Civil War Sites Advisory Commission
> to learn about efforts to preserve the condition of these
> landmarks. At the bottom of this page, you can search all
> Civil War battlefield sites, by campaign or by state, to
> access brief histories, casualty figures, principal comman-
> ders, dates, casualties, and results. Coming soon: the **Civil
> War Soldiers and Sailors System,** which will cull
> information about 5.4 million soldier's records that are
> housed at the National Archives. This will be a multimedia
> demonstration system in partnership with the Archives, the
> African-American Civil War Memorial, the Army Military
> History Institute, and other organizations. To learn more
> about the project, call up the CWSS at (http://www.cr.nps
> .gov/itd/welcome.htm).

Archeology
http://www.cr.nps.gov/archeo.html

> A highlight is an online exhibit, **Ancient Architects of
> the Mississippi,** which recounts the travel of early explor-
> ers and archeological activity in Mississippi, Louisiana,
> Arkansas, and Tennessee. Try out **The National Archeo-
> logical Database,** a communications network for the his-
> torical preservation community.

National Biological Service
http://www.nbs.gov

> Formed in 1993, the National Biological Service is responsible for
> many research programs concerning plants and wildlife. A clickable

Executive Departments

map highlights state-by-state information about programs designed to help protect local flora and fauna.

A Biologist's Guide to the Internet
http://www.nfrcg.gov/home-page/htmls.html

An especially comprehensive topical index of biological sites online.

North American Breeding Bird Survey
http://www.mbr.nbs.gov/bbs/bbs.html

Graphs, range maps, and population analyses of North American birds, organized by species, with common and Latin names. Go to **Songs of Common North American Birds** for clips of dozens of species. The **Patuxent Bird Quiz** challenges you to identify birds by their songs, range, and photo.

Center for Urban Ecology
http://www.nbs.gov/nbs2/cuehome

A team of scientists and technicians is studying the ecology of landscapes influenced by human activities. Program areas include site evaluation, pest management, and urban wildlife.

Bureau of Indian Affairs
http://info.er.usgs.gov/doi/bureau-indian-affairs.html

BIA serves the Indian tribal governments and Alaska Native village communities, and manages 53 million acres of land held in trust for Native Americans by the United States. BIA funds 182 elementary and secondary schools, many operated by tribes under arrangement with the Bureau. Addresses and phone numbers of twelve regional offices are listed here. Indian landowners seeking to manage and develop their natural resources should consult the **Division of Energy and Mineral Resources** (http://snake2.cr.usgs.gov).

U.S. Geological Survey
http://www.usgs.gov

The agency in charge of assessing and conducting research on the nation's land, water, energy, and mineral resources is best known for its wonderful maps and cartographic data.

National Mapping Information (http://www-nmd.usgs.gov) is your gateway to finding the full range of maps; most can be ordered through the **Earth Science Information Center** (http://www-nmd.usgs.gov/esic/esic.html). ESIC is "the map store" for planetary, topographic, aerial photograph, digital, and other kinds of maps, books, and related products. Call (800) USA-MAPS for locations to buy them or order them by mail. **Educational Resources** (http://www-nmd.usgs.gov/www/html/1educate.html) features a number of free posters, booklets, and teaching packets which are available through USGS. Teachers: click on "What Do Maps Show" to find four step-by-step lessons for upper elementary and junior high school classes ready to be downloaded, along with accompanying maps and activity sheets.

At the **National Geospacial Data Clearinghouse** (http://edcwww.cr.usgs.gov/nsdi/digital2.htm), take a few minutes to download the digital satellite map of the United States that greets your arrival. It's one of the most beautiful images we encountered anywhere in our research. Similar digital images are available here and through the Earth Resources Observatory System (EROS) Data Center.

At **The Learning Web** (http://www.usgs.gov/education/index.html), two sections, "Teaching in the Learning Web" and "Living in the Learning Web," explore topics that affect people in everyday life. You can e-mail a scientist and have all your geology questions answered, such as "Why does California have so many quakes?" and "Why is there oil in Texas but not in Wisconsin?" The e-mail address is Ask-A-Geologist@usgs.gov. Parents and teachers should be sure to call up the USGS pathfinder for K–12 Earth Science education.

Geological and Geophysical Research (http://geology.usgs.gov), another USGS site, is the authoritative source on earth's major hazards.

Best Clickable Maps

Bureau of Labor Statistics Regional Information
(http://stats.bls.gov:80/regnhome.htm)

Department of Energy Research Labs
(http://www.doe.gov/html/doe/infolink/usdoemap.html)

Federal Reserve System
(http://www.clev.frb.org/fedlinks.htm)

Forest Service
(http://www.fs.fed.us/recreation/map.htm)

National Network of Libraries of Medicine
(http://www.nnlm.nlm.nih.gov)

National Network of Regional Educational Laboratories
(http://www.nwrel.org/national/regional-labs.html)

National Park Service
(http://www.nps.gov/parklists/pickstates.html)

U.S. AID Regional Information
(http://www.info.usaid.gov/welcome/imap/imap.html)

Learn about earthquakes, volcanoes, landslides, and other geological phenomena at these sites:

National Earthquake Information Center
http://wwwneic.cr.usgs.gov

Find out the latest data on seismic activity anywhere in the world. Be sure to click on Products and Services to see samples of remarkable full-color seismicity maps and posters and how to order them. From here, you can link to the **National Landslide Information Center** (http://gldage.cr.usgs.gov/html_files/nlicsun.html).

Cascades Volcano Observatory
http://vulcan.wr.usgs.gov

> The story of the 1980 Mt. St. Helens eruption, with links to the Alaska and Hawaii volcano labs.

Marine and Coastal Geology Program
http://marine.usgs.gov

> Click on **Highlights** and you'll get extraordinary images that include animations of coastal ocean motion.

Water Resources of the United States
http://h2o.usgs.gov

> USGS is more than rock and maps; it has the principal responsibility for providing hydrologic information and for appraising the nation's water resources. When we signed on, this well-addressed site had extensive information on the controlled flooding of the Grand Canyon.

Executive Departments

DEPARTMENT OF JUSTICE

http://www.usdoj.gov

> The nation's largest law firm serves as counsel for its citizens. DOJ also administers the primary crime-fighting units—the DEA and the FBI—and features the authoritative source on crime statistics, the National Criminal Justice Research Service. The website was under construction when we did our research, so, for now, we'll simply list the addresses for key departments within DOJ, centering on its two most prominent groups, the Litigation Organizations and the Investigatory and Law Enforcement Offices. By the time this edition is in hand, hypertext documents and further information may well be available to you.

Litigation Organizations

Antitrust Division
http://gopher.usdoj.gov/atr/atr.htm

Civil Division
http://gopher.usdoj.gov/civil/civil.html

Civil Rights Division
http://gopher.usdoj.gov/crt/crt-home.html

Criminal Division
http://gopher.usdoj.gov/criminal/criminal-home.html

Environment and Natural Resources Division
http://gopher.usdoj.gov/enrd/enrd-home.html

Tax Division
http://gopher.usdoj.gov/tax/tax-home.html

U.S. Attorneys
http://gopher.usdoj.gov/usao/usao.html

Investigatory and Law Enforcement Offices

Drug Enforcement Administration
http://www.usdoj.gov/dea/deahome.htm

Federal Bureau of Investigation
http://www.fbi.gov

Federal Bureau of Prisons
http://www.usdoj.gov/bop/bop.html

U.S. Marshals Service
http://www.usdoj.gov/bureaus/usm.html

At the **DEA** site are new findings about illegal substances, quantities and value of imported banned substances, arrests of drug lords, and similar information.

It used to be in your post office, but now the Ten Most Wanted Fugitives List is online at the **FBI** home page, with the names, photos/sketches, and crime details of the fugitives. You'll also find online an FBI fact sheet, the latest on the Unabomber and Oklahoma bomb cases, a list of all FBI field offices, rewards offered in current unsolved cases, and the monthly *Law Enforcement Bulletin.*

The **Bureau of Prisons** oversees the 100,000 people committed to the custody of the U.S. Attorney General. At the **Office of Research and Evaluation,** you can access yearly prison statistics and addresses of all correctional institutions as well as an excellent set of links to criminology sites outside the federal government. Call up the Fact Card and you'll get charts and graphs of the total population in federal prisons, broken down by gender, security level, race, type of offense, and cost of confinement. At **UNICOR,** you'll find an online catalog of products (e.g., office furniture) made by inmates.

Office of Justice Programs
http://www.ncjrs.org/ojphome.htm

The Office of Justice Programs supervises five bureaus: (1) Bureau of Justice Assistance, (2) Bureau of Justice Statistics, (3) National Institute

Executive Departments

of Justice, (4) Office of Juvenile Justice and Delinquency Prevention, and (5) Office for Victims of Crime. Its major contribution is the **Justice Information Center** (http://www.ncjrs.org), the most extensive source of information on criminal and juvenile justice in the world, and a clearinghouse for all the programs cited above. From there, you can link to these topic-specific sites: Corrections, Courts, Drugs and Crime, Juvenile Justice, Law Enforcement, and Victims.

One of OJP's newest home pages is the **Bureau of Justice Statistics** (http://www.ojp.usdoj.gov/bjs), where you can find the latest data on firearms, homicide, drug-use rates, capital punishment, comparative statistics of crime rates in other countries, and much more.

Partnerships Against Violence
http://www.usdoj.gov/pavnet.html

Also known as **Pavnet Online,** this is an important interagency electronic resource, a "virtual library" of information about violence and youth-at-risk. Data are contributed by seven different federal agencies. On the Pavnet menu, you'll find more than 125 federal and foundation funding sources, and more than 500 program descriptions and contact sources.

DEPARTMENT OF LABOR
http://www.dol.gov

> The Department of Labor, created in 1913, is charged with preparing the American workforce for new and better jobs and ensuring the adequacy of the workplace. It oversees employment training as well as pensions and employee benefits programs.

Bureau of Labor Statistics
http://stats.bls.gov

> The authoritative source for all data relating to labor—earnings, unemployment, consumer price index, direct investment, employment projections, and more. Click on **BLS Data** to access the most popular data sets (hours, earnings, employment/unemployment rates), or construct your own data sets: compare your earnings or hours with those workers in your field nationally and/or by state and region. Click on **Economy at a Glance** for a nifty table that lays out, over time, employment statistics, hours, earnings, output per hour, consumer price index, and producer price index statistics. Go to **Regional Information** for a stunning clickable map that accesses regional data. And click on **Surveys and Programs** for the latest consumer price indexes and data on employment/unemployment. One of its most well-known publications is the **Occupational Outlook Handbook** (http://stats.bls.gov:80 /ocohome.htm). What's the right career choice for you? Highlights of this standard reference include population and labor force trends, and the job outlook for the year 2005. Parts of this book are online, as are sources for state and local job outlook information.

Employment and Training Administration
http://www.doleta.gov

> A vital source for information about jobs, employment services, unemployment benefits, youth training, and senior service employment programs, plus these career resources:

America's Job Bank
http://www.ajb.dni.us

> A computerized network links the 1,800 state employment
> service offices and provides job seekers with "the largest
> pool of active job opportunities available anywhere." Go to
> Menu Search to access the Job Bank by job type and state.

America's Labor Market Information System
http://ecuvax.cis.ecu.edu/~lmi/lmi.html

> Produced with the support of the Labor Department,
> ALMIS aims to be a one-stop access point for employment
> and training programs nationwide. Among its features will
> be an electronic "talent bank" where employers can search
> a pool of resumes.

School-to-Work Opportunities
http://www.stw.ed.gov

> A joint project of the Education and Labor Departments, to
> prepare young people for high-wage, high-skill careers.

The Occupational Information Network
http://www.doleta.gov/programs/onet/onet_hp.htm

> ONET is expected to be the primary source of occupational
> information and will replace the Dictionary of Occupational
> Titles. It will identify and describe important information
> about occupations, worker skills, and training requirements.

Occupational Safety and Health Administration
http://www.osha.gov

> OSHA's publication office offers numerous online publications, pam-
> phlets, and guidelines to help employees and employers improve work-
> place safety (e.g., "Employee Workplace Rights and Employer Rights
> and Responsibilities").

Pension and Welfare Benefits Administration
http://www.dol.gov/dol/pwba

> PWBA protects the integrity of pensions and employee benefits for more than 200 million people. Especially useful is the six-page document, "Top Ten Ways to Beat the Clock and Prepare for Retirement."

Best Sites for Really Useful Consumer Information

Consumer Information Center (free and low-cost publications) (http://www.pueblo.gsa.gov)

Health Care Financing Administration (The Medicare/Medicaid Agency) (http://www.hcfa.gov)

Genealogy Information (National Archives) (gopher://gopher.nara.gov:70/11/genealog)

Library of Congress LOCIS and Z39.50 Searches (http://lcweb.loc.gov/homepage/online.html)

Name Frequency Database (http://www.census.gov/genealogy/www/freqnames.html)

National Health Information Center (http://nhic-nt.health.org)

Where to Write for Vital Records (certificates of birth, death, marriage, divorce) (http://www.cdc.gov/nchswww/w2w-all.htm)

PAVNET (Partnerships Against Violence) Online (http://www.usdoj.gov/pavnet.html)

Catalog of Federal Domestic Assistance (http://www.gsa.gov/fdac)

Your Post Office (postage rates, zip codes, etc.) (http://www.usps.gov/postofc/pstoffc.htm)

WINGS (Web Interactive Network of Government Services) (http://www.wings.usps.gov/index.html)

DEPARTMENT OF STATE

http://www.state.gov

The State Department, in cooperation with the University of Illinois at Chicago, has created DOSFAN—the Department of State Foreign Affairs Network. This is an excellent site to find information on more than 170 countries with whom Uncle Sam has diplomatic relationships and any of the 260 embassies, consulates, and missions maintained by the U. S. government around the world.

Department of State Gopher

gopher://dosfan.lib.uic.edu

The most valuable information at State can be found at the DOSFAN gopher. Here are a few file folders well worth viewing:

▶ **Publications and Reports.** Researchers, educators, and students will find an enormous breadth of material in "Background Notes," a series of very detailed reports about almost every country in the world, from Afghanistan to Zambia—the politics, history, culture, and trade.

▶ **Contacts and Key Numbers.** Under the Directory of Personnel, you can get the phone numbers of any State Department employee. Under Key Officers List, you can get names and titles of personnel in top positions at all foreign service posts (ambassador, charge d'Affaires, economic officer, legal attache, among others). This information is extremely useful for any person or company doing business overseas.

▶ **Historic and Declassified Documents.** The series, *Foreign Relations of the United States,* is an ongoing compendium of historical documents relating to foreign policy dating back to the Lincoln Administration prepared by the department's Office of the Historian.

Executive Departments

Summaries of some of the newer volumes (e.g., Southeast Asia, 1961–1963) and the full text of a few new volumes are online. Historical documents and declassified minutes of meetings at the White House, the CIA, and the Defense and State Departments are also available.

▶ **Business Affairs.** Here is where you access the "Country Commercial Guides" for almost every country with which the United States maintains diplomatic relations. Each online guide provides essential information about business opportunities overseas, including annual reports on the individual country's political climate, economic trends, investment climate, trade regulations, marketing strategies, and business travel. Under Argentina, for example, we learned of the influence of the Mexican devaluation of the peso on its political and economic system, the names and numbers of five Argentinian law firms with English-speaking lawyers and tax accountants, and the top twenty business prospects for U.S. investment (the top four: tourism, electric power generation, telecommunications, oil and gas field machinery).

Bureau of Consular Affairs/Travel Information
http://travel.state.gov

Perhaps the finest source of international travel information to be found anywhere on the World Wide Web. Find out everything you need to know about passport and visa requirements and how to apply for the necessary documents. Before going overseas, be sure to consult the **Travel Warnings and Consular Information Sheets,** where you'll find an alphabetical guide to the countries of the world and learn of any current problems which may affect your plans, such as military conflicts or outbreaks of disease. You'll also learn about embassy and consulate information, customs data (including the amount of currency that can be brought into and taken out of the country), medical facilities, and tourist tips. (The State Department Travel Warnings are maintained by St. Olaf College in Minnesota which has a sister site—

(http://www.stolaf.edu/network/travel-advisories.html)—with similar and often more timely information.) At **Travel Publications,** access the official State Department literature on subjects ranging from "Tips for Older Americans" to tips for safe travel in the Caribbean, Central and South America, the Middle East and North Africa, Russia and the newly independent states, China, and South Asia. Under **Private American Citizens Living Abroad,** we learned that, in 1995, there were more than three million civilians residing overseas, for whom the most popular locations were Mexico City (350,000 people), Toronto (250,000), London (200,000), and Israel (98,000). Another useful site is **International Adoption**, which offers guidelines to adopting children in scores of foreign countries.

Best Encyclopedias of International Relations

Army/Library of Congress Country Studies
(http://lcweb.loc.gov/homepage/country.html)

CIA World Factbook
(http://www.odci.gov/cia/publications/95fact/index.html)

State Department Commercial Guides and Country Notes
(http://dosfan.lib.uic.edu/www/about_state/about.html)

BEMS (Big Emerging Markets)
(http://www.stat-usa.gov/itabems.html)

Countries Where Peace Corps Volunteers Serve
(http://www.peacecorps.gov/www/io/country1.html)

Greater Horn Information Exchange
(http://www.info.usaid.gov/HORN/index.html)

DEPARTMENT OF TRANSPORTATION

http://www.dot.gov

The jurisdictions of DOT, which was formed in 1967, include highway planning, urban mass transit, railroads, aviation (and air traffic control), and the safety of waterways, ports, highways, and oil and gas pipelines. Find out where to complain about airplane noise in your community, whether your make of car has been recalled, and the latest data on crash tests at the National Highway Traffic Safety Administration. The best-developed and most visually arresting site is one most people would expect to find at the Department of Defense—the Coast Guard.

The U.S. Coast Guard

http://www.dot.gov/dotinfo/uscg

Click on **Coast Guard Areas** and you can access any one of the Guard's units nationwide. At the **Navigation Center** (http://www.navcen.uscg.mil), one especially cool site is the Global Positioning System, a satellite-based radio navigational tool that lets land, sea, and airborne users determine their exact position any time, in any weather condition. **The Coast Guard Auxiliary** (http://131.230.57.1) has terrific consumer information, including e-mail addresses of Coast Guard personnel and a gateway to scores of other boating and sailing pages on the world wide web.

　　U.S. Coast Guard Academy (http://www.dot.gov/dotinfo/uscg/hq/uscga/uscga.html), located on the Thames River in New London, Connecticut, commissions approximately 175 ensigns every year. Cadet life, admissions requirements, and the available academic and military programs are described.

Bureau of Transportation Statistics

http://www.bts.gov

As the name of this division implies, everything you want to know about trains, planes, and other modes of transport. The most useful

Executive Departments

sites are the **Office of Airline Information,** where you can find on-time statistics for every major airline between selected cities, and the **National Transportation Library**, which has good information on bicycles, parking, and congestion management, and lots of safety tips.

Federal Aviation Administration
http://www.faa.gov

At the **Office of Public Affairs,** find out where to complain about aircraft noise, low-flying aircraft, baggage losses, and similar problems. Two hotlines are operative: FAA's Consumer Hotline (1-800-FAA-SURE) and the Safety Hotline (1-800-255-1111). Perhaps the best feature here is the set of links to a dozen or more commercial airlines and airports.

Federal Transit Administration
http://www.fta.dot.gov

Links to mass transit sites such as **Amtrak,** the **New York Subway System,** and **San Francisco Bay Area Transit.** Pick a city, choose your destinations from a list, and request the site to map out a subway route. Commuters, look for several real-time traffic maps displaying up-to-the-minute traffic information by means of detectors placed at strategic points within urban centers. Just a few cities—Houston, Los Angeles, Chicago, San Diego, and Seattle—are up and running so far.

The National Highway Transportation Safety Administration
http://www.nhtsa.dot.gov

Traffic safety is the number-one concern here. The **Research and Development Division** (http://www.nhtsa.dot.gov/nrd/index.html) has an online database of all completed crash tests, sorted by make/model and date of test. Consult the **Consumer Complaints Database** (http://www.nhtsa.dot.gov/nsa/nsasearch.shtml) for complaints about car components and tires, or to reach a recall database or a summary of technical and safety procedures recommended by all auto manufacturers. At the **NHTSA Library,** you'll learn that, in 1994, there were 40,676 deaths in motor vehicle crashes, up 1.3 percent from the year before. Of those, 16,589 were alcohol-related crashes, the lowest number in many years. There were 2,304 motorcycle fatalities in 1994, twenty times the fatality rate of passenger cars per 100 million vehicle miles.

DEPARTMENT OF THE TREASURY

http://www.ustreas.gov

Go to the Treasury Department page and you'll have easy access to all twelve bureaus, including the Bureau of Alcohol, Tobacco and Firearms, the Secret Service, and the Bureau of Printing and Engraving, but you'll find little more than a mission statement at any of these individual sites. We'd like to know more about the Secret Service, the Customs Service, and the Financial Crimes Enforcement Network. On the other hand, call up the IRS and you may think Treasury hired one of the lesser writers from "Saturday Night Live" to design and write copy for its pages. Before we get to the IRS, we'll highlight two bureaus that have some interesting items.

U.S. Mint

http://www.usmint.gov

The Mint Gift Collection, which sells coins and coin sets, jewelry, cuff links, earrings, and watches. For example, you can order a hundred 1979 uncirculated Susan B. Anthony one-dollar coins, in a souvenir bag, for $110.00. Orders can be placed by phone (800-USA-MINT), fax, or mail, using an online order form.

U.S. Customs Service

http://www.ustreas.gov/treasury/bureaus/customs/customs.html

The highlight here is the home page of **Seized Property Auctions** (http://www.ustreas.gov/treasury/bureaus/customs/tas.html) featuring real estate, cars, boats, and jewelry confiscated by either IRS or Customs. Recently, options included a luxury bayfront condominium in San Francisco; five acres of land in Pine Plains, New York; and a prime Lake Tahoe lakefront property, with five bedrooms, one caretaker's house, and two guest cottages on 3.2 wooded acres, with a tennis court and a private pier. The latter's estimated market value was $4.8 million, with a minimum bid required was just over $1 million. Under Date of Sale, a message read, "Auction date has been extended until further notice."

Internal Revenue Service
http://www.irs.ustreas.gov

A mailbox surrounded by nimbus clouds greets you with these words, "Open Here for Some Exciting News. . . ." The IRS's new home has updated electronic services featuring downloadable forms and lots of tax advice. "So pour yourself a cup of coffee, open your mailbox and enjoy our premier issue!"

Whereupon you meet **The Digital Daily** ("Faster than a speeding 1040-EZ"), featuring newspaper headlines like this: "It Pays to Stay in Good Shape with Your Taxes" and "Woman from Lake Cedar Gets Off the Hook by Filing Her Taxes On-Line."

Here are three of the most useful IRS stopovers:

Electronic Services
http://www.irs.ustreas.gov/prod/elec_svs/index.html

> Go here to find out whether you are eligible for this option. CD-ROMs of IRS tax forms are available from the Government Printing Office. Order them here.

Tax Trails
http://www.irs.ustreas.gov/prod/ind_info/tax_trails/index.html

> Quoting again from Uncle Sam: "You'll be sitting pretty for sure when you see that the questions listed below can be answered simply and swiftly. Just follow the trail to the associated prompts." Tax Trails is an interactive session featuring questions like "Can You Claim a Dependency Exemption?" Or, "Can You Include Your Child's Income on Your Tax Return?" Or, "Is My Interest Fully Deductible?" Each has a hypertext link.

Site Tree
http://www.irs.ustreas.gov/prod/search/site_tree.html

> This is your place to saddle up for downloading the forms you need. Almost all forms are accessible here.

So, that's the New, Improved IRS. A word of caution: We had an up-and-down—or, we should say, a Jekyll-and-Hyde—experience trying to download some of the documents and forms, and some of the instructions led us to believe our accountant might still be necessary.

Executive Departments

DEPARTMENT OF VETERANS AFFAIRS
http://www.va.gov

"To care for him who shall have bourne the battle and for his widow and orphan." Abraham Lincoln's epigram introduces the home page of the Department of Veterans Affairs, which provides programs for 70 million eligible citizens. Included are summaries of benefits programs and eligibility requirements, and research on medical and social issues of interest to veterans. Online is the complete contents of the **Veterans Benefits Manual** (http://www.va.gov/publ/benman96). From the home page, click on **VA Facilities** and you'll have a list of 800 numbers for further information, as well as a state-by-state list of the 171 medical centers run by the Veterans Health Administration. Many of the hospitals have separate websites. Each is listed with information on its programs and services, and the names of persons to contact for further information.

Persian Gulf Veterans' Illness
http://www.va.gov/health/environ/persgulf.htm

Call the VA Persian Gulf Veterans Information Hotline at (800) PGW-VETS and consult the resources here. A complementary home page at DOD is called **GulfLINK,** the Persian Gulf War Illnesses Homepage (http://www.dtic.dla.mil/gulflink).

The Traumatic Stress Homepage
http://www.long-beach.va.gov/ptsd/stress.html

An enormous set of resources on post-traumatic stress disorder (PTSD) was created and is maintained by the PTSD Program of the Department of Psychiatry, Carl T. Hayden Veterans Administration Medical Center, in Phoenix, Arizona.

VA Online: The VA Bulletin Board

telnet://vaonline.va.gov

This telnet site overlaps some of the material available through the home page, including the newest edition of the Veterans Benefits Manual, with frequently asked questions and daily benefits announcements and updates.

A unique feature is the **Vietnam Veterans Memorial Database.** All of the names on the Vietnam Veterans Memorial, on the Washington Mall, are searchable by name, state, or hometown. Each entry provides the rank, branch of service, date of birth, casualty date, and panel/line location of the name on The Wall.

CENTRAL INTELLIGENCE AGENCY

http://www.odci.gov/cia

No secrets here. But you will find a great deal of the history of the agency, and one of the finest educational tools in Uncle Sam's back-yard—the World Factbook, a topical encyclopedia of the nations of the world. It's a handsomely devised home page, with a nice tour of the Langley, Virginia headquarters, so spy buffs and foes will enjoy cruising a number of other aspects of the site.

CIA Publications

http://www.odci.gov/cia/publications/pubs.html

Among the items on the bookshelf, use the Intelligence Factbook to find out how to get a job with the CIA or a list of maps available to the public. Read the monthly "Chiefs of State" to find out who's who in the governments of foreign countries. The Chief Historian of the CIA has produced fine pages devoted to biographies of current and past Directors of Central Intelligence (DCIs) and Deputy DCIs, beginning with Major General William J. Donovan, the first head of the Office of Strategic Services (OSS), the forerunner of the CIA.

Independent

CIA World Factbook

http://www.odci.gov/cia/publications/95fact/index.html

One of the best resources in the world of online services. It's a guide to the political, economic, environmental, and geographic situation of most territories and countries in the world, from Afghanistan to Zimbabwe. Clipperton Island (a French possession just twelve times the size of the mall in Washington, D.C.) is even included. Each entry provides a simple map with key cities/towns, an overview of political leaders, religions, population, life expectancy, and the legal system.

The content for the book is provided by a host of institutions: American Geophysical Union, Bureau of the Census, Defense Intelligence Agency, National Science Foundation, and Defense Mapping Agency.

CONSUMER PRODUCT SAFETY COMMISSION

http://www.cpsc.gov

The Consumer Product Safety Commission has a mandate to "protect the public against unreasonable risks of injuries and deaths associated with consumer products." With jurisdiction over 15,000 types of products, the Commission may set voluntary industry standards and produce timely reports (made available to the public) on product hazards. (To subscribe to the e-mail list and automatically receive these reports, send mail to info@cpsc.gov for details.) Through CPSC's gopher, publications on issues ranging from toy safety to carbon monoxide can be retrieved and downloaded. Consumers are urged to report unsafe products via a toll-free Hotline, (800) 638-2772, or by e-mail at info@cpsc.gov.

Independent

CORPORATION FOR PUBLIC BROADCASTING

http://www.cpb.org

Assuming it survives proposed budget cuts, the Corporation will continue to allocate federal funds to public radio and television stations, and various programs being produced for broadcast across the country. This site offers an online version of its annual report and a great guide to public broadcasting online resources—National Public Radio and member stations of PBS, the Public Broadcasting Service. The highlight is **Public Broadcasting Online Directory** (http://www.cpb.org/directory/home.html) which has complete addresses and phone/fax numbers for all Public Broadcasting stations, programs, and networks. If you want to complain about or compliment a particular program or station, or get online sites for your favorite shows and e-mail addresses for people and shows throughout the country, the Directory is all you need.

ENVIRONMENTAL PROTECTION AGENCY

http://www.epa.gov

The Environmental Protection Agency has constructed a very well organized, easy-to-use home page. Since many of its programs are handled at a local level, one of the most useful sites at EPA is at **Regional Offices** (http://www.epa.gov/epahome/Regions.html) where a clickable map accesses all local programs. Browse EPA's **GILS** service (http://www.epa.gov/gils) to find an enormous range of publications and topical information.

Independent

Highly Recommended

http://www.epa.gov/epahome/highly.html

> A guide to the most frequently requested consumer information and technically oriented material. Click on **You and the Environment** and read and/or download eight consumer publications such as "A Citizen's Guide to Pest Control" and "Do's and Don't Around the Home." Under Environmental Issues, access the **Acid Rain** and **Ozone Layer** home pages. And **Environmental Data,** drawn from four EPA programs, gives you a mountain of data on toxic chemicals and hazardous waste.

Access EPA

http://www.epa.gov/Access

> Access EPA is organized like a book of eight chapters. Most vital is Chapter 3, **Clearinghouses and Hotlines,** where the hotline listings provide names, addresses, and phone numbers of personnel to answer your questions on radon, safe drinking water, and similar concerns. Free brochures are usually available.

EPA Publications

http://www.epa.gov/epahome/publications.html

> The gateway to EPA's National Center for Environmental Publications and Information, where you can search, view, and download the most popular of the agency's 5,500 publications. Consumer and professional categories are offered.

Office of Water
http://www.epa.gov/OW

> Find out about national and local programs that seek to protect the
> Chesapeake Bay, the Great Lakes, the national wetlands, and our ocean
> coastal waters. Be sure to visit the beautiful home page at the **National
> Estuary Program** (http://www.epa.gov/nep/nep.html) where a clickable
> map links you to scores of estuaries in four regions: Gulf of Mexico,
> Northeast, South Atlantic, and West Coast. Recent issues of the pro-
> gram's newsletter, *Coastlines,* are also online.

Office of Air and Radiation
http://www.epa.gov/oar/oarhome.html

> Everything you ought to know about the ozone layer, acid rain, indoor
> air quality (radon, for example), automobile pollution, and more. An
> enormous amount of valuable information, including free publications
> and money-saving tips on using household appliances, can be found
> through many sites here.

Independent

THE EXPORT-IMPORT BANK
http://www.exim.gov

The Ex-Im Bank, as it's called, was created in 1934 as a stimulus to economic activity and employment. In the post World War II era, the Ex-Im Bank helped U.S. companies participate in the reconstruction of Europe and Asia. Its aim today is to aid in financing and facilitating U.S. exports. Find out about bank loans and guarantees, eligible markets, and how to finance your products and services overseas.

FEDERAL COMMUNICATIONS COMMISSION
http://www.fcc.gov

The Federal Communications Commission regulates U.S. and international communications by radio, television, satellite, and cable. Profiles and policy statements of the five commissioners, as well as the FCC's seven regulatory bureaus (the Wireless, Cable Service, and Common Carrier bureaus are best known) can be accessed here.

Independent

FEDERAL DEPOSIT INSURANCE CORPORATION

http://www.fdic.gov

The Federal Deposit Insurance Corporation was established by the Banking Act of 1933 to insure banks against collapse. The FDIC's up-to-date statistics on banking and real estate trends can be accessed directly from the home page. Through its gopher, you can access a section on **Consumer Rights.**

FEDERAL EMERGENCY MANAGEMENT AGENCY

http://www.fema.gov

FEMA is best known as the agency that provides financial assistance in the event of a disaster. But its range of activities extends to building code management, emergency preparedness, and administration of flood and crime insurance programs. FEMA provides what it calls a "risk-based emergency management program of mitigation, preparedness, response and delivery." Click on the **Master Index** to access a complete contents of sites.

Independent

Preparing for a Disaster
http://www.fema.gov/fema/predis.html

> Fact sheets encompass each major type of disaster: Natural Disasters (Earthquakes, Extreme Heat, Floods, Hurricanes, Winter Storms, Lightning) and Technological Disasters (Terrorism, Hazardous Materials, House and Building Fires). Safety tips abound in all FEMA's material.

National Flood Insurance Program
http://www.fema.gov/fema/finifp.html

> An excellent guide to myths, facts, and participating insurance companies (by state and in alphabetical order).

Disaster Application Center
http://www.fema.gov/fema/dac.html

> What you need to know if you suffer losses in a disaster: whether you're eligible for disaster assistance, how to apply, and so on. Learn what steps you can take to mitigate the effects of floods, fires, tornadoes, earthquakes, and extreme heat.

Library
http://www.fema.gov/fema/library.html

> A wide selection of online brochures, for example, "How to File a Flood Insurance Claim" and "Emergency Management Guide for Business and Industry." **The Photo Library** (http://www.fema.gov/fema/photo.html) offers pictures from the most recent disasters across the country.

Global Emergency Management System
http://www.fema.gov/fema/gems.html

> GEMS is an index of state and federal resources, including firefighting and search-and-rescue groups.

Government Money

Every year, Uncle Sam gives out billions of dollars in grants, direct payments, insurance, loans, and loan guarantees. Here are a few programs to pursue:

Direct Loan Program (Department of Education)
(http://www.ed.gov/offices/OPE/DirectLoan)

FEMA's Help After A Disaster Page
(http://www.fema.gov/fema/help.html)

Food Assistance Programs
(http://www.usda.gov/fcs/fcsinfo.htm)

National Endowment for the Humanities Grants
(http://www.neh.fed.us/documents/over.html)

National Science Foundation Grants
(http://www.nsf.gov/nsf/homepage/grants.htm)

SBA Small Business Loans
(http://www.sba.gov/business_finances/FinancingYourBusiness.html)

Small Business Administration Disaster Loans
(http://www.sbaonline.sba.gov/DISASTER)

Social Security Benefit Information
(http://www.ssa.gov/programs/programs_intro.html)

Independent

FEDERAL RESERVE SYSTEM

The Federal Reserve System oversees the nation's banking system. Several of the twelve regional Federal Reserve Banks have sites on which you can retrieve reports and papers that give information about the local and national economic scene as well as educational materials; at the San Francisco bank, for example, you'll find curricula materials and video programs available at no cost to high school and junior college teachers. An ideal place to start your search is at the clickable map of the **Twelve Federal Reserve Districts,** accessible through the Cleveland district at (http://www.clev.frb.org/fedlinks.htm).

Federal Reserve Bank of Atlanta

http://www.frbatlanta.org

Federal Reserve Bank of Boston

http://www.bos.frb.org

Federal Reserve Bank of Chicago

http://www.frbchi.org

Federal Reserve Bank of Cleveland

http://www.clev.frb.org

Federal Reserve Bank of Dallas

http://www.dallasfed.org

Federal Reserve Bank of Minneapolis
http://woodrow.mpls.frb.fed.us

The Minneapolis division is named after President Woodrow Wilson, who signed the Federal Reserve System into law. Download software that calculates whether a family or person qualifies for a mortgage under the Community Reinvestment Act, or browse through links to other banking and finance resources. Begin with **About the Federal Reserve,** where there's a good FAQ about the Fed. At **Consumer Information,** you'll find good info on bank mutual fund investments (including glossaries and a complaint line). At **Tracking the Economy,** *The Beige Book* is online summarizing the latest economic conditions; check the latest wage, price, housing start, and employment data, and review interest and exchange-rate charts. And, at **Publications,** read monthly newsletters and reports about banking and lending for consumers and businesses, e.g., "The Credit Process," and "Home Mortgages: Understanding the Process and Your Rights to Fair Lending."

Federal Reserve Bank of New York
http://www.ny.frb.org

If you are knowledgeable about Wall Street or a sophisticated investor, you'll want to keep this address close by. Get access to the latest interest rates and the dates of upcoming T-bill auctions. Check out the Savings Bond Redemption Calculator, where you can punch in information about your savings bonds and the Fed calculates their redemption value instantly. A state-of-the-art website.

Federal Reserve Bank of Philadelphia
http://www.libertynet.org/~fedresrv/fedpage.html

Featured here is the Livingston Survey, which, since 1946, has conducted a national survey of economists' expectations.

Federal Reserve Bank of St. Louis
http://www.stls.frb.org

> Meet FRED (Federal Reserve Economic Database), the bank's database, which has a potpourri of financial statistics—GDP (gross domestic product), Consumer Price Index, monetary data, and so on—compiled daily, weekly, monthly, and quarterly.

Federal Reserve Bank of San Francisco
http://www.frbsf.org

FEDERAL TRADE COMMISSION
http://www.ftc.gov

> The Federal Trade Commission is responsible for antitrust actions and consumer protection. One of the best sites at this watchdog of the public weal is **Consumer Line** (http://www.ftc.gov/bcp/conline/conline.htm) where you can read or download scores of publications ranging from income tax preparation services to fire detection devices and consumer credit issues, and even take a Consumer Quiz.
>
> Each month, the FTC chooses a new topic for discussion (a recent choice was shopping by telephone and mail) and then answers your questions, posting them online. E-mail your own question to consumerline@ftc.gov. At a site called **Consumer Alert! Online Scams** (http://www.ftc.gov/bcp/scams01.htm), learn how to avoid telemarketing and other types of frauds and hazards on the information superhighway.

GENERAL SERVICES ADMINISTRATION

http://www.gsa.gov

The equivalent of Uncle Sam's department store, GSA is the clearing-house for consumer information and for procurement of thousands of commercial items (computers, office equipment and supplies) at the lowest possible prices for U.S. government employees. If you work for Uncle Sam, be sure to consult **GSA Advantage** from the home page. You'll be introduced to an online shopping service reserved exclusively for you and your coworkers. To find out whether you qualify for partici-pation in this service, call the GSA at (703) 305-7359 or e-mail GSA.Advantage@gsa.gov. You can browse a sales brochure and order online at this address—if you have an Activity Address Code (AAC). To apply for an AAC, go to the online application form.

Consumer Information Center

http://www.pueblo.gsa.gov

GSA is home to this famous government cubbyhole. Headquartered in Pueblo, Colorado, CIC publishes and makes available no- or low-cost publications on nearly every subject under the sun—cars, housing, health, jobs, small business, and so on. CIC is well known because it used to devote enormous resources to television and other advertising. Alas, that marketing program is no longer funded, but this website serves a similar function.

CIC offers pamphlets, brochures, and multimedia products on subjects gathered from many different departments. Most of them are readable online and all can be ordered in paper versions by using the toll-free number or downloading an order form. With another online form, request a copy of the complete catalog.

Independent

The CIC's Most Popular Publications
http://www.pueblo.gsa.gov/top20.htm

A terrific convenience is this separate site for the CIC's twenty most popular publications. Half are available for free (e.g., "Protecting Your Privacy," "New Food Label Close-Up," "An FDA Guide to Nonprescription Drugs"). The other half are priced from $.50 to $3.50 (e.g., "Federal Benefits for Veterans and Dependents," "Nine Ways to Lower Your Auto Insurance," "Helping Your Child with Homework").

Federal Information Center
http://www.gsa.gov:80/et/fic-firs/fichome.htm

Have you ever tried to find an answer to a simple question about the federal government and been given a runaround? FIC is, or may be, the remedy. Its service is designed to either answer your specific question or tell you where in the federal government you can have it answered. We wish it were that easy. Call 1-800-688-9889 to give it a try.

Catalog of Federal Domestic Assistance
http://www.gsa.gov/fdac

A compendium of federal programs that provide benefits or assistance to the American public. The entire catalog is available for purchase in different formats from the GSA at the address given here. You can query the catalog with a search function; we typed in "student aid," and got back a list of fifty programs to pursue.

Office of Property Disposal
http://www.gsa.gov/pbs/pr/prhome.htm

If you are interested in buying real estate or other types of property owned by the federal government, this page lists what is available and states the rules for acquisition.

U.S. Government TTY Directory
http://www.gsa.gov/et/fic-firs/ttynbrs/ttyhome.htm

The Telecommunications Accessibility Enhancement Act of 1988 assigned the GSA the responsibility of making the federal telecommunications system fully accessible to individuals who are deaf, hard of hearing, or speech-impaired. This superb site is a clickable gateway that enables those individuals to access most departments in every branch of government.

Government Information Xchange
http://www.info.gov

At the **Federal Yellow Pages,** you'll find an index of hundreds of government agencies arranged by eleven topics, including: business, information technology, workplace, health, money, and military, a feature similar to the **U.S. Business Advisor** at the **White House.** The **Federal Directory** links you to almost every agency and executive office of government. Other links include Foreign Government, International Organizations, and Electronic Shopping Networks.

Independent

NATIONAL ACADEMY OF SCIENCES
http://www.nas.edu

Chartered by Congress in 1863, this private, nonprofit society of scholars advises the federal government on scientific and technical matters. The National Academy of Engineering, the Institute of Medicine, and the National Research Council are among its prestigious divisions. NAS has an excellent array of online books that grapple with questions such as: Are pesticide residues in food harmful to children? What can be done to create more energy-efficient cars? What is the best way to measure poverty? What should the nation's children be learning about science in school? Visit these must-see sites:

A Career Planning Center
http://www2.nas.edu/cpc/index.html

A "one-stop shopping center" for job openings and guidance for beginning scientists and engineers. Are you looking for a mentor, a job, a fellowship, an internship, or postdoctoral work? Or are you an employer looking for a potential employee who has a science and engineering background? Registration is required. If you're a teacher or educator at any level, be sure to visit the following site.

Reinventing Schools
http://www.nap.edu/nap/online/techgap/welcome.html

A state-of-the-art website. The name is taken from the title of a book, *Reinventing Schools: The Technology Is Now,* by Philip M. Smith, former Executive Officer of the National Research Council. Scroll through topics such as **Networking K–12 Education, Learning about Learning, The Role of Government,** and **Multimedia Exhibits,** offered by a consortium of private and public organizations.

Independent

NATIONAL AERONAUTICS AND SPACE ADMINISTRATION

http://www.nasa.gov

If Uncle Sam charged admission to NASA's website, the U.S. government might be out of debt soon. Adjectives cannot describe the breadth of information and history, the extent of resources, or the startling visual images that are now accessible with a modem and the click of a mouse. Full justice cannot be done to NASA in these pages—or via pre-21st-century web technology, even with a 28.8 fax modem and a 17-inch monitor. Uploading, say, the latest photographs from the Hubble telescope can be slow, and cries out for display at an IMAX theater, like the one at the Smithsonian Air and Space Museum. And yet, the pleasures are many, and we've done our best to condense this mammoth site. Make many visits to this great treasure.

If you're new to NASA, you might begin by clicking on the **Welcome, Q&A,** and **Today@NASA** pages for an overview. We've organized your search by combing through all the NASA Centers, such as the Jet Propulsion Laboratory and the Kennedy Space Center, because that's where you'll gain access to almost everything you'll want to see—the history of the Apollo program, the Galileo and Shuttle space missions, the Pluto mission of the future. Illustrations and photographs can be found almost everywhere. And the best is yet to come: NASA is a leader in developing animated and real-time movies for the World Wide Web, so be sure to consult the sidebar called "Uncle Sam Goes to the Movies" for a guide to some of the first and best videos.

For a taste of NASA's best, sample these exceptional sites.

Welcome to the Planets!
http://stardust.jpl.nasa.gov/planets

Tour all the planets and the remarkable vehicles that took the pictures—Mariner 10, Viking, Voyager, Magellan, Galileo, and the Space Shuttle—all from the comfort of your home.

Independent

Hubble Space Telescope (HST)
http://stsci.edu/EPA/Pictures.html

> The best and the brightest of Hubble's incredible portfolio. Hubble is maintained by the **Space Telescope Electronic Information Service** (http://www.stsci.edu/top.html) where you'll find an enormous amount of background information, including the scientific instruments aboard HST.

NSSDC Photo Gallery
http://nssdc.gsfc.nasa.gov/photo_gallery

> What is your pleasure? A planet, a comet, an asteroid, a galaxy, a solar system? Take your pick and enjoy this show, hosted by the National Space Science Data Center.
>
> Now, with those images and a sense of the possibilities in store for you at NASA, here are specific sites to encounter.

NASA Headquarters
http://www.hq.nasa.gov

Office of Legislative Affairs
http://www.hq.nasa.gov/office/legaff

Information about recent happenings in Congress that affect NASA, with links to congressional, governmental, and other policy resources on the web.

NASA Public Affairs
http://www.nasa.gov/hqpao/hqpao_home.html

In the NASA **Newsroom,** get a status report on the events of the day on the ground and up in space, including biographies of key NASA officials and astronauts. Under **Events,** learn how you can watch a space shuttle launch live; you can even arrange for a NASA scientist or engineer to speak to your group or school, courtesy of the NASA Speakers Bureau. **Questions and Answers** provides a top ten list of questions received by NASA (e.g., Do UFOs really exist?). **Spacelink** connects teachers and parents to educational resources. In the **History** section, students and researchers will find an invaluable timeline of air and space developments from 1915 to the present. At **Apollo 11** (http://www.nasa.gov/hqpao/apollo_11.html), relive the first moon landing with movies, astronaut recollections, and historic documents, and audio files ("One small step . . .").

Office of Space Flight
http://www.osf.hq.nasa.gov

A fantastic page design introduces you to a number of must-see sites, among them: the **Space Hotlist** (NASA's choice for what's cool), the **Space Station Mir** and, our favorite, **All U.S. Human Space- flights,** which is the most comprehensive source for background on the Mercury, Gemini, Apollo, and Skylab missions.

Office of Life and Microgravity Sciences and Applications
http://mercury.hq.nasa.gov/office/olmsa

Among its many missions: to explore the scientific phenomena that can only be tested in the very low gravity of space, and to develop advance spacesuit and life-support technologies to sustain humanity's quest in space.

Mission to Planet Earth
http://www.hq.nasa.gov/office/mtpe

Fulfills NASA's mandate to explore Earth from outer space, focusing in particular on climatic change.

Independent

Office of Space Science
http://www.hq.nasa.gov/office/oss

Uses robotic spacecraft to understand the Sun, the solar system, the Milky Way, and the Universe. This is your gateway to **The Sun–Earth Connection** (Space Physics) and **Structure and Evolution of the Universe** (Astrophysics).

Office of Procurement
http://www.hq.nasa.gov/office/procurement

A list of current NASA procurement opportunities, with links to procurement offices at NASA's many research centers.

Office of Space Communications
http://mercury.hq.nasa.gov/office/spacecom

How does NASA keep track of probes and spaceflights in outer space? The **Ground Networks** Page describes the various facilities that allow Earthlings to keep in touch with outer space.

NASA Technical Reports Service
http://techreports.larc.nasa.gov/cgi-bin/NTRS

A terrific service for researchers and specialists in all scientific fields. Access any of thousands of abstracts that are located throughout the NASA network. Enter a search topic and do parallel searches at two or more of fifteen NASA centers connected to this service. For example, we typed in "Shoemaker-Levy" (the name of the comet that hit Jupiter) and were presented with almost a hundred abstracts to choose from for further reading. A related site is **NASA Scientific and Technical Information Program** (http://www.sti.nasa.gov/STI-homepage.html), which features thousands of electronic documents; one related site we would especially recommend is the **NASA Video Catalog** (http://www.sti.nasa.gov/videocat/_COVER.htm).

NASA's Educational Resources

All of NASA's websites are educational, but many have been designed expressly for K–12 teachers and students. Here are some of the best of them. For a comprehensive list, be sure to consult **NASA Internet Educational Resources** (http://quest.arc.nasa.gov/OER/EDRC22.html).

Quest! The K–12 Internet Initiative
(http://quest.arc.nasa.gov)

At Quest, you can participate in online discussion groups. Recent projects have included **Online from Jupiter,** which tracked the progress of Galileo in late 1995, and **Live from the Hubble Space Telescope.** Learn about aerospace resources on the Internet with the link to **Route 66**, a catalyst (non-NASA) site that links to perhaps the most comprehensive list of K–12 servers on the World Wide Web.

The Space Educators' Handbook
(http://tommy.jsc.nasa.gov/~woodfill/SPACEED/SEHHTML/seh.html)

An electronic interactive space encyclopedia. The home page begins, "One small click for all mankind . . . ." Learn about the missing day in time, the death of a star, how volcanoes were discovered on Jupiter's moon, the lives of Kepler and Newton. The Space Educators' Handbook is available as a HyperCard 2.1 program for use on Apple Mac computers or as a Window ToolBook 1.5 program. It includes related files interactively linked for ease of learning about NASA, space science, and space technology. Copies are available to educators; for further information, consult this site. For younger kids, check out Space Comics, download, and put those colored pencils to work. And be sure to check the "Hidden Cool Stuff."

Independent

NASA's Educational Resources *(continued)*

Space Link
(http://spacelink.msfc.nasa.gov)

Aptly described as "An Electronic Information System for Educators." Scores of instructional materials and lesson plans; a Teacher Resource Center; and links to electronic conferences, some of which are live and feature NASA scientists as guest speakers. You can set up your own conferences to discuss topics of your choice. Includes a Spacelink Educator Directory that can identify other account holders geographically. E-mail addresses are provided to facilitate communication among educators.

Space Science Education Page
(http://www.gsfc.nasa.gov/education/education_home.html)

For younger astronomers, an introduction to astrophysics and planetary science. Click on "Lessons" and you'll find a stunning home page with links to all the planets, with fact sheets, a history of missions, and a planetary photo gallery. Click on "Curricula Materials" and you'll find a Teacher's Resource Lab. Another good bet is **Ask Dr. Sue**, who wants to bring the excitement of astronomy and earth science into the classroom. Students can communicate by e-mail with NASA's Dr. Sue Hoban (Susan.Hoban@gsfc.nasa.gov).

The JASON Project
(http://seawifs.gsfc.nasa.gov/scripts/JASON.html)

The JASON project was founded in 1989 by oceanographer Dr. Robert D. Ballard, following his discovery of the *Titantic*. The goal is to enable teachers and students to take part in global explorations, using advanced interactive telecommunications. The focus in on grades 4 through 8. Consult the Teachers' Guide and Students' Corner to fully appreciate the educational possibilities and how to apply the program in your classroom.

Just for Fun!
(http://www.gsfc.nasa.gov/education/just_for_fun/fun_home.html)

Separate space fact from fiction and learn about the science of *Star Trek*.

Independent

NASA's Educational Resources *(continued)*

Amazing Facts
(http://pao.gsfc.nasa.gov/gsfc/earth/efacts/efacts.htm)

About the earth—that is, arranged under the headings Our Oceans, Our Atmosphere, Our Land Surfaces. A sample topic: Using the theory of plate tectonics, scientists say that Southern California will collide with Alaska in approximately 150 million years!

Telescopes in Education Project
(http://encke.jpl.nasa.gov/TIE/TIE_index.html)

Designed to encourage interest in astronomy among K–12 students, the program allows students and amateurs to remotely work the telescope at Mt. Wilson. Take a pop quiz: Can you identify astronomical objects? is a sample.

The STELLAR Experiential Teacher Education Program
(http://stellar.arc.nasa.gov)

STELLAR stands for Science Training for Enhancing Leadership and Learning through Accomplishments in Research—a hands-on science training program for K–12 teachers. Teachers from San Francisco Bay area schools are chosen to work side-by-side with NASA scientists each summer, but there's a lot for everyone else to learn. Lesson plans include Could Martian Water Support Life? and Hydroponics: Growing Without Soil.

NASA Programs for Individuals
(http://university.gsfc.nasa.gov/individual.html)

The NASA Academy is a summer institute of higher learning for graduate and undergraduate students in the physical sciences, engineering, math, and computer science. This is just one of many programs for students to learn about.

Independent

NASA's Educational Resources (continued)

Basics of Space Flight Learners' Workbook
(http://www.jpl.nasa.gov/basics)

An introduction to the solar system (asteroids, comets, the sun) and more.

Atlas of Mars
(http://fi-www.arc.nasa.gov/fia/projects/bayes-group/Atlas/Mars)

Features a "virtual spacecraft" to view the globe of Mars from almost any position, with six to eight levels of zoom.

The TOPEX/POSEIDON Project
(http://topex-www.jpl.nasa.gov)

The Ocean Topography Experiment is a cooperative project between the U.S. and France to operate a satellite system dedicated to observing the earth's oceans. The goal is to develop global maps of ocean topography to better predict global climate. There are cooperative home pages of this project at other NASA sites, all accessible here.

SAREX—Shuttle Amateur Radio Experiment
(http://www.gsfc.nasa.gov/sarex/sarex_mainpage.html)

A long-running program to use amateur radio equipment on board the Space Shuttle, allowing the astronauts in orbit to answer questions transmitted by amateur radio operators.

Exploration in Education
(http://stsci.edu/exined-html/exined-home.html)

ExInEd is a NASA-supported program at the Space Telescope Science Institute, home to the Hubble Space Telescope. Electronic PictureBooks are on display (most of them for Macs only) featuring "Gems of Hubble 2.0," "The Planetary System," "Volcanic Features of Hawaii," and "Images of Mars."

NASA's Educational Resources *(continued)*

Youth Enhancing Space Project (formerly KidSat)

(http://www.jpl.nasa.gov/kidsat)

Go to space without leaving the ground. A three-year pilot program designed to give younger science students the chance to take photos and study Earth's atmosphere from the Space Shuttle.

The ILIAD Library Project

(http://www.jsc.nasa.gov/stb/ILIAD/Mosaic/iliad.html)

ASK ILIAD searches the World Wide Web for answers to e-mail questions. It originated with elementary and secondary teachers at the Texas Education Network who had limited computing resources.

HPCC K–12 Activities at Lewis Research Center

(http://www.lerc.nasa.gov/Other_Groups/K-12/K-12_homepage.html)

HPCC stands for High Performance Computing and Communications. This program is designed to increase the computer literacy of K–12 students. Learn how some schools have put this program to use, for example, in a "Wandering Wind Tunnel Project."

Views of the Solar System

(http://bang.lanl.gov/solarsys)

An educational tour of the solar system, with images and information about the sun, planets, moons, asteroids, comets, and meteoroids. Over 970 high-resolution images and animations, and over 840 megabytes of data. Statistical information can be browsed through sorted lists. Learn about rocket history, early astronauts, and a detailed chronology in The History of Space Exploration. This page was compiled by Calvin J. Hamilton of the Los Alamos National Laboratory.

Independent

Official Space Shuttle Homepage
http://shuttle.nasa.gov

On the first NASA Shuttle mission of 1996 (and the 74th for the Space Shuttle Program), *Endeavor* and its six-person crew retrieved a Japanese satellite, deployed and retrieved a NASA science satellite, and conducted two space walks. Here's where you could have accessed the countdown clock, NASA-TV, and crew and landing information. Stay tuned for the next Shuttle mission.

Ames Research Center
http://www.arc.nasa.gov

Ames was founded in 1939 as an aircraft testing center by the National Advisory Committee for Aeronautics, the predecessor to NASA. Situated on 430 acres in the heart of California's "Silicon Valley," Ames has branched into many different research areas, including supercomputing and artificial intelligence, and is home to the world's largest wind tunnel and several advanced flight simulators. Be sure to stop by the **Space Science Division** (http://www-space.arc.nasa.gov /division/main.html), the R&D arm of Ames, which is dedicated to the understanding of the origin and evolution of stars, planets, and life. The home page illustration alone, representing "the host of natural phenomena which collectively have created life as we know it" is worth the visit.

Center for Mars Exploration
http://cmex-www.arc.nasa.gov

Click on the Mars Educational Multimedia CD-ROM and you can fly a virtual spacecraft over the martian surface. Extraordinary images here, and a worthy complement to **Mars Exploration,** at the Jet Propulsion Laboratory site (described later in this listing).

Commercial Technology Electronic Network

http://ctoserver.arc.nasa.gov

Background on products that Ames scientists believe are ripe for commercialization; a link to the **Ames Technology Commercialization Center,** which assists small businesses based on NASA technology.

Dante II

http://maas-neotek.arc.nasa.gov/dante

Meet Dante, a robot with the mission of exploring dangerous and unsafe worlds. Over the course of several months in 1994, Dante explored the inside of an Alaskan volcano. Find out what the robot beamed back and the implications of the sojourn for robotics and space exploration. Unfortunately, Dante fell into the inferno and the project has been concluded.

Pioneer Project

http://pyroeis.arc.nasa.gov/pioneer/PNhome.html

The first spacecraft to fly past Jupiter. Pioneer 10 and Pioneer 11 were significant contributors to NASA's solar system studies. Learn about the missions, history, and current status.

Asteroid and Comet Impact Hazard

http://ccf.arc.nasa.gov/sst

Are you worried about something big, fast, and hot hitting the Earth? Then this is the page for you. Get the latest surveys on the probability of a comet or asteroid hitting the Earth, a list of **Near Earth Objects,** meteorite movies, and impact images, plus links to similar sites.

The Planetary Rings Node

http://ringside.arc.nasa.gov

Everything you ever wanted to know about the rings of Saturn, Jupiter, Uranus, and Neptune, plus photos and animations.

Independent

Galileo Probe

http://ccf.arc.nasa.gov/galileo_probe

Galileo, which started its journey on October 18, 1989 with the launch of the Space Shuttle Atlantis, visited Jupiter from December 1995 to March 1996. Preliminary analysis of data has provided startling discoveries for project scientists.

Dryden Flight Research Center

http://www.dfrc.nasa.gov/dryden.html

NASA's premier installation for aeronautical flight research; located at Edwards Air Force Base, California, on the edge of the Mojave Desert. One of its missions is support of the Space Shuttle program as a primary and backup landing site.

Since the days of the X-1, the first aircraft to fly faster than the speed of sound, Edwards AFB has been associated with many milestones, including supersonic flight, wingless lifting bodies, fly-by-wire, and the Space Shuttle.

Goddard Space Flight Center

http://pao.gsfc.nasa.gov/gsfc.html

Goddard Space Flight Center, created in January 1959, was named for Dr. Robert H. Goddard, the American pioneer in rocket research. The Center's mission is to expand knowledge of the Earth and its environment, the solar system, and the universe, through observations from space. Located in Greenbelt, Maryland, it is also the "nerve center" for the Hubble Space Telescope, the command post for all data gathered at the Space Telescope Operations Control Center.

Independent

Space Science
http://pao.gsfc.nasa.gov/gsfc/spacesci/spacepic.htm

Look at the inside of a nebula, watch stars being born, and explore the Milky Way. This gallery offers, with explanatory notes, some of the best recent pictures taken by Hubble. Link here to the **Space Telescope Science Institute** (http://www.stsci.edu/stci.html) which maintains the world's largest catalog (twenty million entries) of images of the entire night sky. The **STSCI Catalogs and Surveys Branch** can be found at (http://www-giss.stsci.edu/casbhome.htm).

Large Scale Phenomenon Network of the International Halley Watch
http://eyes.gsfc.nasa.gov

An extensive database of information and images taken during the return of Halley's comet, 1981–1989. A set over 1,400 pictures arranged by date on eighteen CD-ROMs and available for viewing online.

Solar Data Analysis Network
http://umbra.nascom.nasa.gov/sdac.html

Watch solar eclipses and see photos and movies from the most recent solar eclipses around the world.

National Space Science Data Center
http://nssdc.gsfc.nasa.gov

The deep archive for NASA planetary and lunar data. You can perform searches on the databases for the kind of images you want—even photos of astronauts living in space. Teachers: don't miss the **Space Science Education** page (http://ssdoo.gsfc.nasa.gov/education /education_home.html) where you'll find lessons and curricula materials in astrophysics, planetary science, and space physics.

Independent

Goddard Institute for Space Studies
http://www.giss.nasa.gov

A subdivision of the Goddard Space Flight Center, GISS is primarily engaged in studies of global climate change. Founded by Dr. Robert Jastrow in 1961, GISS is located on the campus of Columbia University in New York City.

Jet Propulsion Laboratory
http://www.jpl.nasa.gov

Managed for NASA by the California Institute of Technology, and located in Pasadena, California, JPL is the lead U.S. center for robotic exploration of the solar system. JPL spacecraft have visited all known planets except Pluto. (A Pluto mission is now under consideration for the late 1990s.) JPL also manages the worldwide and wonderfully named Deep Space Network, which communicates with spacecraft.

Planetary Exploration
http://www.jpl.nasa.gov/mip/planet.html

An overview of JPL's many past and present missions and spacecraft—Mariner, Voyager, Galileo, and Viking—and a hint of the future and the planned Pluto Express.

Imaging Radar
http://southport.jpl.nasa.gov

An extraordinary site for learning about radar with stunning images and movies of earth and space. Begin at the **First Time Visitors** page, and don't miss a clickable map of the world at (http://southport.jpl .nasa.gov/imagemaps).

Independent

Comet Observation
http://encke.jpl.nasa.gov

Information and illustrations of comets currently visible. The great comet of 1996, **Hyakutake,** has its own home page at (http://www.jpl.nasa.gov/comet/hyakutake).

Comet Shoemaker-Levy
http://www.jpl.nasa.gov/sl9

From July 16 through July 22, 1994, the comet known as Shoemaker-Levy crashed into Jupiter. This was the first collision of two solar system bodies ever to be observed. See the exciting photos of the contact.

Project Galileo
http://www.jpl.nasa.gov/galileo

The Galileo spacecraft arrived at Jupiter on December 7, 1995. Learn "Amazing Galileo Facts" and link to other Galileo-related home pages. This is one of the most popular home pages in NASA's domain and understandably so.

Voyager Project
http://vraptor.jpl.nasa.gov/voyager/voyager.html

Voyager 1 and Voyager 2 sped by most of the outer planets and are now on their way into the galaxy carrying messages from Earth. Find out what extraterrestrials will learn about Earth from Voyager. Online are recordings of greetings in 55 different languages.

Mars Exploration
http://www.jpl.nasa.gov/mars

The Mars Pathfinder mission plans to send robotic probes to Mars. Meet Rover the robot, and read a newsletter of current developments up there, aptly named *The Martian Chronicle,* "the electronic newsletter for Mars

Independent

Exploration." Two other key Mars sites at JPL are: **Mars Pathfinder** at (http://mpfwww.jpl.nasa.gov) and **Mars Global Surveyor** at (http://mgs-www.jpl.nasa.gov).

New Millennium Program
http://nmp.jpl.nasa.gov

Humankind is no longer earthbound. Future space exploration will be so extensive that a "virtual human presence" will extend throughout the solar system—and beyond. The New Millennium Project takes the first steps toward realization of a new vision of space exploration by developing and validating innovative technologies for future missions.

Space Calendar
http://newproducts.jpl.nasa.gov/calendar

For the astronomically obsessed, be sure to consult the Space Calendar which offers daily space-related events (comets, eclipses, anniversaries), manned or unmanned launches and landings, and lectures and symposia for the coming year. (Tip: On March 27, 1997, Comet Hale-Bopp will make its closest approach to the earth.)

Johnson Space Center
http://www.jsc.nasa.gov

This space center, located in Houston, Texas, is the focal point of international cooperation in human spaceflight. The Space Shuttle and the International Space Station are the two most important programs promoting cooperation.

International Space Station
http://leonardo.jsc.nasa.gov:80/ss

The home page, including photos and animations, of one of the first truly international projects in history. Space partners came from Russia, Europe, Canada, the United States, and other countries.

Astronaut Biographies
http://www.jsc.nasa.gov/Bios/astrobio.html

Searchable biographies of all current astronauts.

Lunar and Planetary Institute
http://cass.jsc.nasa.gov

Check in at Hot Topics to see satellites of the outer planets and 3D images of the moon. LPI also publishes an interesting monthly publication called *Solar System Express* (http://cass.jsc.nasa.gov/sse /sse.html).

JSC Digital Images Collection
http://images.jsc.nasa.gov

Over 250,000 images from Shuttle and previous manned missions have been captured, digitized, and stored. Link here to the **NASA Photo Gallery** which tries to bring all of NASA's still images under one roof.

John F. Kennedy Space Center
http://www.ksc.nasa.gov

The departure point for Project Apollo's manned explorations of the moon, the Kennedy Space Center, on the Florida peninsula, has primary responsibility for ground turnaround and support operations and launch of Space Shuttle missions.

Independent

Tour the Facilities
http://www.ksc.nasa.gov/facilities/tour.html

The highlight is the Vehicle Assembly Building, one of the largest buildings in the world.

Public Affairs
http://www-pao.ksc.nasa.gov/kscpao/kscpao.htm

Up-to-date information on Shuttle launches and landings, various space missions, mission reports for all the past Shuttle missions, factoids about NASA and the Shuttle, and services for educators.

Historical Archive
http://www.ksc.nasa.gov/history/history.html

A superb history of rocketry and manned space travel; examines the launch, crew, and duration of the Mercury, Gemini, Apollo, Skylab, and Space Shuttle missions.

Expendable Launch Vehicle Program
http://www.ksc.nasa.gov/elv/elvpage.htm

Not all space missions are manned and not all satellites are deployed as scheduled. Those "other" missions, many contracted by private companies, are covered under the ELV program. News on upcoming launches and payloads (if they're not classified).

Langley Research Center
http://www.larc.nasa.gov

Established in 1917 as the first national civil aeronautics laboratory, Langley's primary mission is basic research in aeronautics and space technology. Langley, based in Hampton, Virginia, is also the acknowledged world leader in the creation, design, and use of wind tunnels.

Lewis Research Center
http://www.lerc.nasa.gov

> Lewis Research Center, adjacent to Cleveland's Hopkins International Airport, defines and develops advanced propulsion, power, and communications technologies for application to aeronautics and space.

George C. Marshall Space Flight Center
http://www.msfc.nasa.gov

> At this center for mission control activities and research, in Huntsville, Alabama, the home page offers two choices: general information and technical information. From the general information page, find out about types of research being done, get factsheets, tour Huntsville, and check out **Spacelink,** one of NASA's best sites of education resources.
>
> ### Liftoff to Space Exploration
> http://liftoff.msfc.nasa.gov
>
> An introduction to the Shuttle and Space Station resources at Marshall. At **Liftoff Academy** (http://liftoff.msfc.nasa.gov/academy /academy.html) questions and answers about astronomy, space, time, and rocket science; astronaut trivia; and a quiz that changes monthly.
>
> ### Science Research
> http://www.msfc.nasa.gov/general/research.html
>
> Learn about an enormous range of subjects, including biotechnology, astronomy, space physics, and materials science, each of which links to scores of technical and educational resources. One of many interesting sites: **Lightning Detection from Space** (http://wwwghcc.msfc.nasa. gov/lisotd.html).

Independent

Reusable Launch Vehicle Technology Program
http://rlv.msfc.nasa.gov

The RLV program is working to create a less expensive means of sending people and cargo into space. Check out some of the prototypes (in animation and image form) to see how close we are.

John C. Stennis Space Center
http://www.ssc.nasa.gov

The Stennis Space Center, situated in Hancock County, Mississippi, is NASA's primary center for testing large rocket propulsion systems for the Space Shuttle and future generations of space vehicles. It is also NASA's lead center for the commercialization of remote sensing applications. If you think your business could benefit from the use of space-based observation (looking for minerals, coastal monitoring, and so on) see how NASA is working with businesses and providing incentives to investigate the use of remote sensing.

Wallops Flight Facility
http://www.wff.nasa.gov

The Wallops Flight Facility was established in 1945 on Virginia's Eastern Shore under NASA's predecessor, the National Advisory Committee for Aeronautics, for the purpose of conducting aeronautical research using rocket-propelled vehicles. Its first rocket was launched on July 4, 1945. During the halcyon days of manned missions, Wallops led the research effort in reentry and life-support systems. Today, in conjunction with Goddard Space Flight Center, it is NASA's primary facility for suborbital programs, including balloons and aircraft to research the Earth's atmosphere.

Before we depart NASA, we close with our choice of the number 1 site on Uncle Sam's web, an unparalleled, mind-expanding cyber-journey through the universe. It's called **Views of the Solar System** and beneath this single home page you'll find images, movies, and information that will thrill any student, teacher, and novice or expert astronomer, which includes just about everyone. Interestingly, this site was developed not inside NASA but at the Los Alamos Laboratory; its address is (http://bang.lanl.gov/solarsys). We are in debt to webmaster Calvin J. Hamilton for this work of art.

Best Sites to Explore
U.S. History

American Memory (Library of Congress)
(http://lcweb2.loc.gov/amhome.html)

Apollo Manned Space Program (Smithsonian)
(http://www.nasm.edu:80/APOLLO/Apollo.html)

Center of Military History (Army)
(http://imabbs.army.mil/cmh-pg/default.htm)

Charters of Freedom (National Archives)
(http://www.nara.gov/exhall/charters/charters.html)

Civil War Battlefields (National Park Service)
(http://www.cr.nps.gov/abpp/battles/statlist.html)

Historical Archive at the John F. Kennedy Space Center
(http://www.ksc.nasa.gov/history/history.html)

History of Computing (Army Research Lab)
(http://ftp.arl.mil/~mike/comphist)

Smithsonian Archives of American Art
(http://www.si.edu/organiza/offices/archart/start.htm)

Trinity Symposium (Department of Energy)
(http://www2.dp.doe.gov/MapServe/text/TRINITY.HTM)

Independent

NATIONAL ARCHIVES AND RECORDS ADMINISTRATION

http://www.nara.gov

The National Archives preserves and makes available for research the permanently valuable records of the federal government from its beginnings in 1774. Among these records are the Charters of Freedom: the Declaration of Independence, The Constitution, and the Bill of Rights, which are on permanent display in the rotunda of the National Archives in Washington, DC. Other documents include slave ship manifests and the Emancipation Proclamation; journals of polar expeditions; the Louisiana Purchase Treaty; and the records of all our wars. Archives facilities in Washington alone store more than 4 billion pieces of paper and 7 million still photos.

CLIO, named for the muse of history, is the moniker of NARA's online gopher server. Most of the records are not online at this time, so check the site often for updated material.

About the National Archives

http://gopher.nara.gov:70/1/about

A good place to begin learning about the extent of NARA's mission, which includes the Federal Register and online versions of the vast microfilm catalogs ("Immigrant and Passenger Arrivals" and "Military Service Records," for example). Knowing which microfilm you need will speed your research. The **National Archives Fax-On-Demand System** (http://gopher.nara.gov:70/0/about/faxdem.txt) is especially useful for quick access to hundreds of documents available through this service.

Federal Register

gopher//gopher.nara.gov:70/11/register/toc

Those who need to be informed of the quotidian doings of their government will appreciate access to the **Federal Register,** a daily listing of everything that happens in the government. See entry at the Government Printing Ofice.

The U.S. Government Manual
http://www.access.gpo.gov/nara/nara001.html

Uncle Sam's official handbook, the *Government Manual,* provides the most comprehensive guide to the agencies of the legislative, judicial, and executive branches. A typical entry gives the names of principal officials, a summary of the agency's purpose, a brief history, an explanation of its legislative or executive authority, a description of its programs and activities, and a "sources of information" section (which includes consumer activities, contracts and grants, publications, and other areas of public interest).

The *Manual* has a Government Printing Office address, but we include it here because it is produced by NARA and the Office of the **Federal Register.** Use the search function to access departments and individuals.

Genealogy
http://clio.nara.gov:70/genealog

There are two parts to this page: (1) links to other genealogical resources online and (2) a guide to microfilm holdings at the archives. If you want to research your family's history, for example, you probably want to start here with census data, passenger and immigration lists, and military records. The introduction explains how you can get books and pamphlets on genealogical research, and the microfilm catalog listing explains what genealogical resources have been microfilmed and are available for use.

NARA Government Information Locator Service
http://www.nara.gov/gils/gils.html

NARA's GILS is a virtual card catalog of the Archives' information resources. Browse the document titles to learn the voluminous extent of information within NARA and how you can access it.

Independent

Online Exhibit Hall

http://www.nara.gov/exhall/exhibits.html

Some of NARA's holdings are indeed online, and this is one of the finest sites to ascertain what is available. Featured documents, when we checked in, included **The Emancipation Proclamation, The 19th Amendment,** and the **Japanese Surrender Statement** from World War II.

The Charters of Freedom

http://www.nara.gov/exhall/charters/charters.html

If you were to visit the Archives in person, you might have to wait in line for a very brief viewing of these precious documents. Online, you can savor reproductions of them, download them in their entirety, and read scholarly background materials on their origins.

▶ **The Declaration of Independence.** To enrich your understanding, the Archives offers a few articles, including the far less known Virginia Declaration of Rights, which strongly influenced Jefferson's first draft of the Declaration and provided the foundation for the Bill of Rights.

▶ **The Constitution of the United States.** You can call up either a text transcription or a high-resolution image of each of the pages of the original Constitution. An accompanying article, "A More Perfect Union," provides an in-depth look at the Constitutional Convention and the ratification process.

▶ **The Bill of Rights.** The first ten amendments to the Constitution are downloadable as well. An accompanying article, "A Voice of Dissent," tells about George Mason, who had been one of the Constitution's most vocal opponents and was a force toward passage of the Bill of Rights.

Information about Records Retained by Presidential Libraries
http://clio.nara.gov:70/inform/library

The best site for learning the exact contents of archival material in each of the eleven presidential collections.

Presidential Library System
http://clio.nara.gov/nara/president/address.html

Before the advent of the Presidential Library System, presidential papers were often dispersed at the end of each administration and/or lost or destroyed. The Presidential Library System formally began in 1939, when FDR donated his personal and presidential papers to the government and pledged part of his Hyde Park estate to the United States. (The Hoover Presidential Library was created in August 1962 many years after the FDR donation.)

Together, the nine presidential libraries and two presidential projects that comprise the System maintain over 250 million pages of text, 5 million photos, 68,000 hours of disk and audio and video tape recordings, and 280,000 museum objects. This site is your gateway to the presidential resources maintained by NARA. On the home pages, you'll get links to the individual archives, e-mail and mailing addresses, and phone numbers. The home page addresses are listed here in the chronological order of the presidencies.

Herbert Hoover Library
http://sunsite.unc.edu/lia/president/hoover.html

Franklin D. Roosevelt Library
http://www.academic.marist.edu/fdr/fdrintro.htm

Harry S. Truman Library
http://sunsite.unc.edu/lia/president/truman.html

Dwight D. Eisenhower Library
http://sunsite.unc.edu./lia/president/eisenhower.html

Independent

John Fitzgerald Kennedy Library
http://sunsite.unc.edu/lia/president/kennedy.html

Lyndon Baines Johnson Library
http://www.lbjlib.utexas.edu

Nixon Presidential Materials Staff
http://sunsite.unc.edu/lia/president/nixon.html

Gerald R. Ford Library/Museum
http://sunsite.unc.edu/lia/president/ford.html

Jimmy Carter Library
http://sunsite.unc.edu/lia/president/carter.html

Ronald Reagan Library
http://sunsite.unc.edu/lia/president/reagan.html

George Bush Presidential Materials Project
http://csdl.tamu.edu/bushlib/bushpage.html

Most of these libraries' home pages originate at the University of North Carolina at Chapel Hill (UNC), which maintains a presidential home page. Further background, Clinton–Gore Internet Archives, and a First Ladies website are additional features. For a terrific example of an online library exhibit, visit **A Day in the Life of a President** (http://www2.sils.umich.edu/FordLibrary/DayInTheLife.html). Produced by the Gerald R. Ford Library, this exhibit takes the virtual tourist through a day in the life of a U.S. president and shows all the facets of the chief executive's power and roles (commander-in-chief, statesman, ceremonial leader, and so on).

The President John F. Kennedy Assassination Records Collection
http://www.nara.gov/nara/jfk/jfk.html

All the Archives materials related to the assassination of JFK are housed in a single collection at NARA's office in College Park, Maryland, and are searchable online.

NATIONAL ENDOWMENT FOR THE ARTS

http://arts.endow.gov

> NEA was created in 1956 to encourage and support American arts and artists. Learn about grants in creative writing, jazz, and other fields and access a list of more than 60 state and regional arts organizations.

NATIONAL ENDOWMENT FOR THE HUMANITIES

http://www.neh.fed.us

> The NEH sponsors programs and projects designed to enhance knowledge of and interest in all the humanities—language, literature, philosophy, archaeology, comparative religion, and ethics. Through the home page, you'll learn how to apply to NEH grant programs and find links to State Humanities Councils. An index lists films and radio and TV programs receiving NEH funding. **NEH Projects** (http://www.neh.fed .us/documents/online.html) offers access to funded programs ranging from archaeological digs to collections of great books transferred into an electronic form. Another highlight: The Martin Luther King Jr. papers.

Independent

NATIONAL RAILROAD PASSENGER CORPORATION
http://www.amtrak.com

Amtrak's station offers a map and a guide to all its routes. For reservations, use the reliable tool, the telephone, and dial 1-800-USARAIL. Amtrak expects to offer online bookings and reservations by January of 1997.

NATIONAL SCIENCE FOUNDATION
http://stis.nsf.gov

The National Science Foundation's mandate is to promote the progress of science and thereby advance the national health, prosperity, and welfare of the United States. NSF is noteworthy because the Internet originally grew out of NSFNET—a plan to link research and education to various computational resources. NSF awards significant grants and fellowships to promote science education and evaluate new technologies. The site is organized largely by Directorates (e.g., Directorate for Mathematical and Field Sciences, and Directorate for Computer and Information Science and Engineering). You'll find links to most grant, program, and funding areas from the home page.

One of the most consumer-oriented sites at NSF is **Directorate for Education and Human Resources** (http://red.www.nsf.gov), a hugely entertaining guide to Internet science sites, including NSF's own **Science in the Home,** which features interactive projects at the beginner, intermediate, and advanced levels. At the **Office of Polar Program** (http://www.nsf.gov:80/od/opp/start.htm), visit the Arctic region and Antarctica—or at least find out about U.S. research at these remote locations.

Independent

Links to NSF Science and Technology Centers include:

Center for Analysis and Prediction of Storms
http://wwwcaps.uoknor.edu

Center for Computer Graphics and Scientific Visualization
http://www.cs.brown.edu/stc

Center for Particle Astrophysics
http://physics7.berkeley.edu/home.html

Center for Research in Cognitive Science
http://www.cis.upenn.edu/~ircs/homepage.html

Center for Research on Parallel Computation
http://www.crpc.rice.edu/CRPC

Center for Superconductivity
http://www.stcs.uiuc.edu

National Center for Atmospheric Research
http://www.ucar.edu

National Optical Astronomy Observatories
http://www.noao.edu/noao.html

National Radio Astronomy Observatory
http://info.aoc.nrao.edu

Southern California Earthquake Center
http://www.usc.edu/dept/earth/quake/index.html

Independent

National Technology Transfer Center

http://www.nttc.edu

The NTTC was created with a single purpose in mind: to get government research out of laboratories and into the hands of U.S. companies. Its "gateway service" is intended to make it easy for anyone, from large corporations to entrepreneurs working out of their garages, to access the wealth of research sponsored by Uncle Sam. NTTC says on its Program page: "All you have to do is call us and describe the challenge you are dealing with or tell us the technology area you want to explore. Our NTTC Technology Access Agent does the rest—FREE OF CHARGE." The toll-free phone number is (800) 678-6882.

Half a dozen "success stories" of high- and low-tech companies that have done that exploration are cited. In Kansas City, David Porter, the president of Garment Care, Inc, a dry cleaner, was awarded $50,000 to develop a "rack/conveyor system" to carry soiled clothes through an ultrasound bath. You're invited to call Mr. Porter to see whether you can do it too.

Nuclear Regulatory Commission

http://www.nrc.gov

On January 5, 1996, NRC held what may be considered a historic event in the annals of public service. NRC conducted a "real-time" public hearing on fire protection rules at nuclear power plants by linking its website with four Kinko's copy shops around the country that were equipped for web communication. Top NRC officials went to a nearby Kinko's at the same prearranged time that members of the public gathered at the other copy shops. Press accounts of this event reported that the NRC is apt to rely on the participants' comments as it drafts new regulations. Most agencies solicit comments from citizens and have home pages that publish e-mail addresses, but it's always hard to assess the extent to which the public's voices are being heard.

Independent

Peace Corps

http://www.peacecorps.gov

A wonderful opportunity to learn about the history and current status of the Peace Corps, even if you don't want to become a volunteer. Schools can bring the Peace Corps into their classrooms by inviting volunteers to contribute their voices and experiences.

Peace Corps Chronological History

http://www.peacecorps.gov/www/press/Press5.html

The Peace Corps began with an impromptu speech at the University of Michigan by presidential candidate John F. Kennedy, on October 14, 1960, when the future president challenged students to give two years of their lives to help people in the developing world.

Countries Where Volunteers Serve

http://www.peacecorps.gov/www/io/Country1.html

Divided by regions (Africa, Inter-America, Asia-Pacific, and Eastern Europe and the Mediterranean), the country profiles present "Background Notes" and links to other Internet resources about each country.

World-Wise Schools

http://www.peacecorps.gov/www/dp/WWS1.html

Each year, this site links about 4,500 U.S. classrooms to Peace Corps volunteers overseas. Teachers enrolled in the program receive videos and study guides about Peace Corps countries to supplement their geography curriculum. (Study guides can be downloaded through this web server.) Go to **Letters from the Field** (http://www.peacecorps .gov/www/dp/WWSL1.html) to read letters from volunteers overseas.

Independent

Office of Private Sector Relations
http://www.peacecorps.gov/www/opsr/OPSR1.html

> How can your organization or company help the work of the Peace
> Corps? This page describes two programs—Gifts-in-Kind, and Peace
> Corps Partnership Programs—that aim to connect the American public
> to Peace Corps work.

Office of Volunteer Recruitment and Selection
http://www.peacecorps.gov/www/vrs/VRS1.html

> Is the Peace Corps right for you? Find out what skills and qualifica-
> tions are required. Read the FAQ—with 101 Q's and A's—and then
> use an online guide if you decide to apply.

SECURITIES AND EXCHANGE COMMISSION
http://www.sec.gov

The SEC is responsible for administering federal securities laws and protecting investors in securities markets.

What Every Investor Should Know
http://www.sec.gov/invkhome.htm

A number of online guides, primarily for novice investors. Titles include: "Invest Wisely" (actually two guides have the same name; one is about choosing a broker and picking an investment, and the other is an introduction to mutual funds); "What Every Investor Should Know" (the essentials of investing); and "Arbitration Proceedings" (resolving disputes with stockbrokers). Keep an eye out for a forthcoming quiz to test your investment knowledge.

EDGAR Database
http://www.sec.gov/edgarhp.htm

As of May 1996, publicly traded corporations must enter certain filings required by the SEC into the EDGAR database. (EDGAR stands for Electronic Data Gathering, Analysis and Retrieval system.) Some forms need not be submitted, but the valuable 10-K is one of those required. We typed in two companies, Microsoft and Merck, for retrieval, and more than a dozen forms—10-K, 10-Q, 8-K, S-3, and S-8, among others—for the past two years appeared on the screen. We clicked on the 1995 10-K for Microsoft and learned that it was founded as a partnership in 1975 and incorporated in 1981, and that it is divided into four main divisions: Platforms Product Group, Applications and Content Product Group, Sales and Support Group, and Operations Group. We also learned that the corporate offices occupy a little over 2 million square feet in Redmond, Washington, on two sites

Independent

situated on 300 acres of land. The Employee Stock Purchase Plan was displayed, as was a list of all executive officials and the company's revenues for the past year (Microsoft seemed to have had a good year).

On Merck's 10-K, we learned that cardiovascular drugs outsell its second leading category, anti-ulcerants, by better than 3 to 1, and that the next strongest sales categories were, in order, antibiotics, vaccines, opthamologicals, and anti-inflammatories/analgesics. We were told that Merck has a long-term research and marketing collaboration with duPont to develop a new class of therapeutic agents for high blood pressure and heart disease, and that Merck and Johnson & Johnson have a joint venture to sell over-the-counter pharmaceuticals throughout Europe.

In the emerging field of "company intelligence," EDGAR is a gold mine.

SELECTIVE SERVICE SYSTEM
http://www.sss.gov

The mission of the Selective Service System is to deliver untrained man-power to the armed forces in time of emergency and to administer the alternative service program for conscientious objectors.

A system of conscription was used during the Civil War and again during World War I; in both cases the draft mechanism was dissolved at the end of the hostilities. The first peacetime draft in the U.S. history was enacted in 1940 prior to our entry into World War II. From 1948 to 1973, during times of peace and conflict, men were drafted to fill vacancies in the armed forces which could not be filled through voluntary means. Induction authority expired in 1973 but the SSS remained in a "Standby" posture to support the all-volunteer armed forces. Beginning in 1980, the registration requirement resumed. Today, young men must register within 30 days of their eighteenth birthday.

In the event of a mobilization, a lottery drawing would determine the order in which men would be called. The first priority group would be men in the calendar year of their twentieth birthday.

Learn more about the SSS history as well as conscientious objection and women and the draft. Registration forms are available online.

Independent

Ships, Bases, and Forts

Looking for a family member or friend at sea, abroad, or on a base here in the states? Perhaps you just want to know what life is like at the base or on the ship. Here are the addresses for ships, bases, and forts that have their own websites.

Army

Fort Benning (http://www.benning.army.mil)

Fort Bliss (http://bliss-www.army.mil)

Fort Bragg (http://www.bragg.army.mil)

Fort Campbell (http://campbell-emh5.army.mil/campbell.htm)

Fort Carson (http://www.carson.army.mil)

Fort Detrick (http://www.medcom.amedd.army.mil/detrick)

Fort Eustis (http://www.eustis.army.mil)

Fort Gordon (http://www.gordon.army.mil)

Fort Hood (http://www.hood-pao.army.mil)

Fort Huachuca (http://huachuca-usaic.army.mil)

Fort Jackson (http://jackson-www.army.mil)

Fort Knox (http://147.238.100.101)

Fort Leavenworth (http://www-cgsc.army.mil)

Fort Lee (http://cascom-www.army.mil)

Fort Leonard Wood (http://www.wood.army.mil)

Fort McClellan (http://www-tradoc.army.mil/mcclellan)

Fort McCoy-Chapel (http://www.msilbaugh.com/mchapel.htm)

Fort McPherson (http://www.mcphersn.army.mil)

Ships, Bases, and Forts *(continued)*

Fort Meade (http://www.mdw.army.mil/meade.htm)

Fort Monmouth (http://www.monmouth.army.mil)

Fort Monroe (http://www-tradoc.monroe.army.mil/monroe)

Fort Stewart and Hunter Army Airfield (http://158.20.22.136)

Fort Wainwright (http://143.213.12.254/home.htm)

White Sands Missile Range (http://www-wsmr.army.mil)

Navy

USS Blue Ridge (http://www.c7f.yokipc.navy.mil/c7fblu.html)

USS Carl Vinson (http://www.navy.mil/homepages/cvn70)

USS Constitution (http://www.navy.mil/homepages/constitution)

USS Dwight D. Eisenhower (http://www.navy.mil/homepages/cvn69)

USS John C. Stennis (http://www.navy.mil/homepages/jcs)

USS Hawes (http://www.navy.mil/homepages/uss-hawes)

Air Force

Air Combat Command (http://www.acc.af.mil)

Check clickable map at (http://www.acc.af.mil/acc_sites.html)

Barksdale AFB (http://bncc-w3.barksdale.af.mil)

Beale AFB (http://www.beale.af.mil)

Cannon AFB (http://ns2.cannon.af.mil)

Davis-Monthan AFB (http://www.dm.af.mil)

Dyess AFB (http://www.dyess.af.mil)

Ellsworth AFB (http://www.ellsworth.af.mil)

Independent

Ships, Bases, and Forts *(continued)*

Griffiss AFB (http://www.rl.af.mil:8001/Tour/GAFB/Griffiss.html)

Holloman AFB (http://www.holloman.af.mil)

Howard AFB (http://www.howard.af.mil)

Lajes AFB (http://www.lajes.af.mil)

Langley AFB (http://www.langley.af.mil)

MacDill AFB (http://www.macdill.af.mil)

Minot AFB (http://www.minot.af.mil)

Moody AFB, GA (http://www.moody.af.mil)

Mountain Home AFB, ID (http://www.mountainhome.af.mil)

Nellis AFB, NV (http://www.nellis.af.mil)

Seymour—Johnson AFB (http://www.seymourjohnson.af.mil)

Shaw AFB (http://www.shaw.af.mil)

Tinker AFB (http://www1.tinker.af.mil)

Whiteman AFB (http://www.whiteman.af.mil)

Air Education and Training Command (http://www.aetc.af.mil)

Check clickable map at (http://www.aetc.af.mil/AETC-Bases)

Altus AFB, OK (http://www.lts.aetc.af.mil)

Columbus AFB (http://www.col.aetc.af.mil)

Goodfellow AFB, TX (http://www.gdf.aetc.af.mil)

Keesler AFB, MS (http://www.kee.aetc.af.mil)

Lackland AFB, TX (http://www.lak.aetc.af.mil)

Laughlin AFB, TX (http://www.lau.aetc.af.mil)

Independent

Ships, Bases, and Forts *(continued)*

Luke AFB, AZ (http://www.luk.aetc.af.mil)

Maxwell AFB, AL (http://www.aetc.af.mil/AETC-Bases/maxwell.html)

Randolph AFB, TX (http://www.aetc.af.mil/AETC-Bases/randolph.html)

Sheppard AFB, TX (http://www.spd.aetc.af.mil)

Tyndall AFB, FL (http://admin.325lg.tyndall.af.mil/index.html)

Vance AFB, OK (http://www.vnc.aetc.af.mil)

Air Force Materiel Command (http://www.afmc.wpafb.af.mil:12000)

Arnold AFB, TN (http://info.arnold.af.mil)

Brooks AFB, TX (http://www.brooks.af.mil)

Edwards AFB, CA (http://www.elan.af.mil)

Eglin AFB, FL (http://www.eglin.af.mil)

Hanscom AFB, MA (http://www.hanscom.af.mil)

Kelly AFB, TX (http://www.kelly-afb.org)

Los Angeles AFB, CA (http://www.laafb.af.mil)

McClellan AFB, CA (http://www.mcclellan.af.mil)

Newark AFB, OH (http://www.newark.af.mil)

Robins AFB, GA (http://www.robins.af.mil)

Tinker AFB, OK (http://www1.tinker.af.mil/default.htm)

Wright-Patterson AFB, OH (http://www.wpafb.af.mil)

Independent

Ships, Bases, and Forts *(continued)*

Air Mobility Command (http://www.safb.af.mil/hqamc/pa)

Scott AFB, IL (http://www.safb.af.mil)

Travis AFB, CA (http://www.travis.af.mil)

Pacific Air Forces (http://www.hqpacaf.af.mil)

Andersen AFB, Guam (http://www.andersen.af.mil)

Eielson AFB, AK (http://icebox.eielson.af.mil)

Elmendorf AFB, AK (http://www.topcover.af.mil)

Kadena AB, Okinawa (http://www.kadena.af.mil)

Kunsan AB, Korea (http://www.kunsan.af.mil)

Osan AB, Korea (http://www.osan.af.mil)

Pearl Harbor, HI (http://www.pac.disa.mil)

Yokota AB, Japan (http://www.yokota.af.mil)

United States Air Force Europe (http://www.usafe.af.mil)

Aviano AB, Italy (http://www.avi.af.mil)

Einsiedlerhof AS, Germany Warrior Preparation Center
(http://www.wpc.af.mil)

RAF Lakenheath, UK (http://www.usafe.af.mil/bases/laken/laken.htm)

Sembach AB, Germany (http://www.sembach.af.mil)

Spangdahlem AB, Germany (http://www.spangdahlem.af.mil)

SMALL BUSINESS ADMINISTRATION
http://www.sba.gov

> The SBA was created in 1953 to assist and protect small business concerns.

Starting Your Business
http://www.sba.gov/business_management/StartingYourBusiness.html

> Through workshops, publications, counseling, and videotapes, SBA helps entrepreneurs deal with the many facets of a start-up—financing, marketing, management, and so on. Access those products here, as well as a guide to 100 field offices nationwide. Two other good sources are the Service Corps of Retired Executives (SCORE), comprised of more than 13,000 volunteers, and 600 Small Business Development Centers.

Financing Your Business
http://www.sba.gov/business_finances/FinancingYourBusiness.html

> The SBA helps small business secure capital. At this site, you get background on scores of loan programs as well as downloadable applications. There's even a proposal preparation handbook.

Expanding Your Business
http://www.sba.gov/business_expansion/ExpandingYourBusiness.html

> Matching the advice on start-up and financing, this site provides help for entering and succeeding in the global marketplace. Counseling by international trade experts, publications, and Matchmaker Trade Missions (cosponsored by the Department of Commerce) can link U.S.

Independent

firms with potential foreign buyers. Featured here is a state-by-state list of prime contractors' names, products, and services; it is also an excellent source of subcontracting opportunities.

Regional Offices

http://www.sbaonline.sba.gov/regions/regionmap.html

Use the clickable color map to pick any state and gain access to a range of data on local SBA offices, SCORE personnel, and Preferred Lenders.

SBA Hot Links

http://www.sba.gov/hotlist

One of the finest indexes in Uncle Sam's domain. Link to Internet sites of special interest to entrepreneurs: the Senate Committee on Small Business, Dun & Bradstreet, *The Wall Street Journal,* to Yahoo's List of Small Business Sites, and more.

Procurement Offices

So your business wants to take advantage of a government contract and do business with Uncle Sam? The **Small Business Administration** (SBA) has a site that advises you just how to sell to the government (http://www.sba.gov/gopher/Government-Contracting). Check out SBA's procurement-related "hotlist" too (http://www.sba.gov/hotlist). Two other gateways are **FinanceNet's** Electronic Commerce Resource Sites (http://www.financnet.gov/ec.htm) and at the **U.S. Business Advisor,** the Selling to the Government Page (http://www.business.gov/DoingBusiness.html#SG).

Other sites to explore:

Defense Acquisition Information
(http://www.dtic.dla.mil/hovlane)

Department of Commerce GLOBUS
(http://www.stat-usa.gov/BEN/Services/globus.html)

Department of Energy Procurement Homepage
(http://www.doe.gov/procure/prpages.html)

Environmental Protection Agency Contracts
(http://www.epa.gov/epahome/Contracts.html)

Federal Acquisition Jumpstation
(http://procure.msfc.nasa.gov/fedproc/home.html)

General Services Administration Electronic Commerce Program Management Office
(http://www.gsa.gov/ecapmo)

Government Printing Office Procurement Services
(http://www.access.gpo.gov/procurement/index.html)

NASA Procurement Homepage
(http://procure.msfc.nasa.gov/nasaproc.html)

NOAA System Acquisition Office
(http://www.sao.noaa.gov/procure.html)

U.S. Air Force Acquisition Page
(http://www.hq.af.mil/SAFAQ)

U.S. Army Acquisitions
(http://www.sarda.army.mil)

Independent

SMITHSONIAN INSTITUTION
http://www.si.edu

It is possible to capture online the essence of The Smithsonian, often referred to as "the nation's attic." In fact, the vastness of cyberspace allows you to tour many of the world's most famous museums in a way that would be impossible during a vacation trip to the nation's capital. Michael Heyman, the current secretary, says in his welcoming statement that he expects "the electronic transformation of the Smithsonian" to be the defining mark of his tenure.

The treasures of the Smithsonian are simply immense. We recommend you begin by clicking on the **Welcome** page, where you learn that the Smithsonian Institution was established in 1846 with funds bequeathed by an English scientist named James Smithson, and that it holds some 140 million artifacts and specimens for "the increase and diffusion of knowledge." The Smithsonian is composed of sixteen museums and galleries and the National Zoo, as well as numerous research facilities in the United States and overseas. Nine of the museums are located on the Washington Mall, five others and the Zoo are elsewhere in the District of Columbia, and the Cooper-Hewitt National Design Museum and the National Museum of the American Indian are in New York City.

You can access almost all these sites through the Welcome page. By clicking on **Places** on the home page, you arrive at an even more highly recommended access point. You'll see that the Smithsonian is divided into four components—museums, research centers, offices, and affiliated organizations—which provide the sequence for our journey through the treasures of the Smithsonian.

Before we start our trip, you should be aware of a feature called **Navigating the Electronic Smithsonian** (http://www.si.edu /electrsi/navigate.htm). Electronic Smithsonian will be the Smithsonian's World Wide Web server—the gateway to everything in the "Nation's Cyber-Attic." Learn about navigation and search tools, icons, and the equipment needed to explore the Smithsonian online. Another terrific introductory feature is **The Encyclopedia Smithsonian** (http://www.si

.edu/welcome/faq/start.htm), which answers visitors' most frequently asked questions on topics ranging from anthropology (e.g., Egyptian mummies and pyramids) to musical history (Stradivarius violins), transportation history (the voyage of the *Titanic*), and zoology (the Loch Ness monster).

In 1996, the Smithsonian marks its 150th anniversary, so it's appropriate that a splendid traveling and online exhibit has been produced. Featuring many of the museum's most treasured objects, the exhibit is divided into three categories: Remembering, Imagining, and Discovering. Access the site from the home page or at (http://www.150.si.edu/150Trav/150Exhib.htm). Another traveling exhibit, which opened at the National Museum of Natural History in April 1995, is **Ocean Planet** (http://seawifs.gsfc.nasa.gov/ocean plant.html). The culmination of a four-year effort, Ocean Planet uses cutting-edge technology and "walk-through" environments to provide a better understanding of conservation of the world's oceans.

Smithsonian Museums

Anacostia Museum
http://www.si.edu/organiza/museums/anacost/start.htm

A national resource for the identification, documentation, protection, and interpretation of African American history and culture. Recent online exhibits include: "Black Mosaic: Community, Race, and Ethnicity Among Black Immigrants in Washington, DC," "The Meaning of Kwanzaa," and "The Renaissance: Black Arts of the Twenties."

Cooper-Hewitt National Design Museum
http://www.si.edu/organiza/museums/design/start.htm

Devoted to the study and exhibition of historical and contemporary design.

Independent

The Freer Gallery of Art

http://www.si.edu/organiza/museums/freer/start.htm

One of the world's most distinguished collections of Asian art, as well as works by such American artists as James McNeill Whistler, including his famous "Peacock Room."

Arthur M. Sackler Gallery

http://www.si.edu/organiza/museums/artsack/start.htm

Devoted to scholarship and exhibition of Asian art. Changing exhibitions include Japanese prints, Persian manuscripts, and Near Eastern gold and silver.

Hirshhorn Museum and Sculpture Garden

http://www.si.edu/organiza/museums/hirsh/start.htm

Nineteenth- and 20th-century modern art and sculpture by Rodin, Calder, Matisse, Giacometti, de Kooning, Dubuffet, Rauschenberg, and others.

National Air and Space Museum

http://www.nasm.edu

This most frequented of all Smithsonian museums dramatizes the history of flight, space science, and space technology. Be sure to visit the **Center for Earth and Planetary Studies** (http://ceps.nasm.edu:2020 /homepage.html). At its **Regional Planetary Image Facility,** you'll find a reference library of photos, images, and maps taken from planetary missions. Using the selection buttons at the bottom you can pick a planet to examine or browse through the collection of Space Shuttle photographs (e.g., satellite photos of the Dead Sea and the Grand Canyon). A huge page of information explains how to order copies of the photos and images; there are links to other online photo archives. Another highlight is the **Apollo Manned Space Program** (http://

www.nasm.edu:80/APOLLO/Apollo.html). Click on one of the color patches to access the history of each moon mission, and learn the Top 10 scientific discoveries of the Apollo program. Students, teachers and researchers will want to stop by the **Department of Space History** (http://www.nasm.edu/NASMDOCS/DEPT_SH.html) which has been conducting oral interviews on the history of space flight and technology from the German V-2 project to the Hubble Space Telescope. Recent exhibits included "Where Next, Columbus?"

National Museum of African Art
http://www.si.edu/organiza/museums/africart/start.htm

Televisit Africa through photos selected from the Eliot Elisofon Photo Archives.

National Museum of American Art
http://www.si.edu/organiza/museums/amerart/start.htm

Exhibitions include Vedder's Rubáiyát of Omar Khayyám and works by Edward Hopper, among others. Especially useful here are the extensive lists of resources for historians and researchers of American art.

National Museum of American History
http://www.si.edu/organiza/museums/nmah/start.htm

Exhibits include the first ladies' inaugural gowns, Ben Franklin's printing press, and a hands-on science center. Coin collectors will take a shine to The National Numismatic Collection, where they can meander through online exhibits about the coinage of ancient Greece, and learn why Corinth was one of the earliest Greek cities to strike and use coins. The 1804 Exhibit highlights rarities recently donated to the collection. The exhibit is named after the 1804 silver dollar, "The King of American Coins," so named because it was minted only to serve as gifts to Asian rulers. Another fine site is **The Innovation Network** (http://innovate .si.edu) which grew out of the Computerworld Smithsonian Awards Program. Founded in 1987, this award program honors visionaries in the fields of medicine, media, education, business, finance, and manufacturing. Online oral and video histories of past winners include: Robert Ballard, Seymour Cray, Bill Gates, Ann Meyer, and Douglas Engelbart. The Innovation Network is a collaborative effort of the Smithsonian, *Computerworld,* and the Novell Corporation.

S. Dillon Ripley Center
http://www.si.edu/organiza/museums/ripley/start.htm

The Ripley Center houses The Smithsonian Associates (the continuing education arm of The Smithsonian) and The International Gallery.

The Smithsonian Institution Building
http://www.si.edu/organiza/museums/castle/start.htm

The original Smithsonian Institution building, completed in 1855 and commonly known as the "Castle," was designed by James Renwick, Jr., who was also architect for St. Patrick's Cathedral in New York City. The Castle houses the Smithsonian's Information Center and the Woodrow Wilson International Center for Scholars.

Arts and Industries Building
http://www.si.edu/organiza/museums/artsind/start.htm

The Arts and Industries Building is the second-oldest Smithsonian building on the National Mall. Completed in 1881 in time for President Garfield's inaugural ball, it was built to display materials from the Centennial Exposition in Philadelphia.

The White House Collection of American Crafts
http://www.nmaa.si.edu/whc/whcpretourintro.html

Far more than an online exhibit of crafts. Visit behind the scenes with the artists and watch them create their masterworks. Learn, for example, how glassblower Josh Simpson made "Megaworld." A wonderful way to learn about crafts using wood, metal, or fiber, or just to explore the diversity of American culture and art.

Independent

Uncle Sam Goes to the Movies

Sometime in the future, maybe next year, maybe in three years, movies on the Net will be customary entertainment. But at this moment in technological history (circa 1996), the files for downloading a movie onto your screen are often enormous (up to 20 minutes download time with a 14.4 or 28.8 modem). The movies that are available can be awesome, especially those at NASA, so it's often worth the effort and your patience.

Before you take your popcorn out of the microwave, your web browser will require some additional video-playing software. You can find links to shareware versions of this software at almost every government location where there are videos. Among the different types of video and video players, most in Uncle Sam's studio are in what is called MPEG format. MPEG videos do not usually feature sound, which lessens the size of the file and the download time. Other formats you'll find include .avi or QuickTime format, which are usually larger files.

NASA Video Gallery
(http://www.hq.nasa.gov/office/pao/Library/video)

Bring your milk duds. This Video Gallery tries to bring NASA's best videos together under one roof. A non-government site to bookmark: the Space Movie Archive (http://www.univ-rennes1.fr/ASTRO/anim-e.html) is arguably the world's largest collection of space animations.

Hubble Space Telescope Animations
(http://www.stsci.edu/pubinfo/Anim.html)

Featured films include: "Rotating Mars Globe," "Evidence of Oxygen on Europa," "Orion Nebula," and "Saturn Storm."

Cassini Spacecraft Movies
(http://www.jpl.nasa.gov/cassini/Moview/index.html)

Watch Cassini on its way to Saturn and the Huygens probe landing on Saturn's moon Titan.

Independent

Uncle Sam Goes to the Movies *(continued)*

Views of the Solar System Images and Animations
(http://bang.lanl.gov/solarsys/raw/index.htm)

Some of the finest films here are from the Apollo missions. On Apollo 11, watch the landing sequence, the first steps on the moon, and the liftoff. On Apollo 13, relive the clip featuring the famous dialogue, "Houston, we've got a problem." On Apollo 14, astronaut Alan Shepard plays golf on the moon.

Jet Propulsion Laboratory Radar Imaging
(http://southport.jpl.nasa.gov/video.html)

Simulated flights around the Galapagos Islands, Death Valley, San Francisco, Los Angeles, and the Lost City of Ubar.

Reusable Launch Vehicle Quick Time Movies
(http://rlv.msfc.nasa.gov/rlv_htmls/RLVMovies.html)

QuickTime videos of prototype reusable launch vehicles. See an actual test launch straight from the famous "Skunkworks."

Dante II Mission Images
(http://img.arc.nasa.gov/Dante/images.html)

MPEG videos of the actual descent of the Dante II robot into the Mt. Spurr Volcanic Crater. Check out the video of what Dante II saw as it met its demise.

National Weather Service Weather Videos
(http://iwin.nws.noaa.gov/iwin/videos/videos.html)

"Twister," move over; here are hurricane, tornado, and flood videos.

Department of Engraving and Printing
(http://www.ustreas.gov:802/treasury/bureaus/bep/bep.html)

Informational videos of web printing presses and money coming hot off the press.

Uncle Sam Goes to the Movies *(continued)*

Snowball Cam Cinema

(http://www.rl.af.mil:8001/Odds-n-Ends/sbcam/rlsbcam.html)

From the Air Force's Rome Laboratory comes the infamous Snowball Cam. Throw virtual snowballs at targets inside the lab to score points and get your name up on the leader board. Watch a double feature, "Snowball Cam: The Movie," billed as a day in the life of the Rome Laboratory Snowball Cam, and "Revenge of the Snowball Cam."

Smithsonian 150th Anniversary Cinema

(http://www.150.si.edu/150trav/cinema/cinema.htm)

Video clips of Native American songs, the playing of a Stradivarius cello and, most notably, the flight of Charles Lindbergh's Spirit of St. Louis.

National Zoo Cinema

(http://www.si.edu/organiza/muscums/zoo/homepage/hilights/cinema.htm)

First there was "The Lion King." Now meet the Golden Lion Tamarins in the National Zoo Cinema, along with the Komodo dragon, the orangutans, and the gorillas.

Library of Congress Early Motion Pictures, 1897–1916

(http://lcweb2.loc.gov/ammem/papr/mpixhome.html)

In a word, wow! A fascinating portfolio of historical films in .avi format. When we took our seats, three collections from the earliest days of film were online, including 26 short films of San Francisco before and after the great earthquake and fire. Another collection, "The Last Days of President McKinley," consisted of twenty-eight short films featuring footage of the president at his second inauguration. These films were produced by the Edison (as in Thomas) Manufacturing Company in 1901. The third exhibition was "The Life of a City: Early New York, 1898–1906."

Independent

National Postal Museum

http://www.si.edu/organiza/museums/postal/start.htm

Home to 14 million stamps—the most comprehensive collection in the world.

National Museum of the American Indian

http://www.si.edu/organiza/museums/amerind/start.htm

The George Gustav Heye Center of the National Museum of the American Indian is located in the Alexander Hamilton U.S. Customs House in lower Manhattan. The complete museum is not scheduled to open on the Mall in Washington until 2001. After viewing the superb online exhibitions, be sure to go to the homepages of **Publications and Recordings** and **Other Native American Sites** for further exploration of the Native American experience.

National Museum of Natural History

http://www.si.edu/organiza/museums/nmnh/start.htm

Browse the exhibits as well as other natural science sites on the Internet. Don't miss **Dinosaur Hall.**

National Portrait Gallery

http://www.si.edu/organiza/museums/portgal/start.htm

Past and current exhibitions are online, illustrated with digitized photos. Recent features were the Hall of Presidents and "Majestic in His Wrath: The Life of Frederick Douglass."

National Zoological Park

http://www.si.edu/organiza/museums/zoo/start.htm

Family entertainment can be found throughout this beautifully developed site. Be sure to click on **Eye on DOI,** a chance to get up close and personal with spiders, insects, and other inhabitants of the zoo's Department of Invertebrates.

Under **Exhibits,** visit the new **Think Tank,** where Orangutans are being taught how to communicate. At the **Great Ape House,** meet the gorillas, including supermom Mandara. Under **Animals and Biological Science,** learn how artificial reproduction is being used to preserve species, watch a movie of the monkeys at the zoo, and relive a giraffe birth. And be sure to enter the **Pollinaurium** to answer these questions: "Why are flowers colorful?" "How do bees make honey?" and "Do insects see colors the way people do?"

Renwick Gallery

http://www.si.edu/organiza/museums/renwick/start.htm

Dedicated to American designers and craftspeople.

Smithsonian Research Centers

Office of Fellowships and Grants

http://www.si.edu/organiza/offices/fellow/start.htm

Information about fellowship and intern programs run by the Smithsonian.

Archives of American Art

http://www.si.edu/organiza/offices/archart/start.htm

The world's largest single source for documentary materials on the visual arts of the United States.

Smithsonian Astrophysical Observatory

http://sao-www.harvard.edu/sao-home.html

Established in 1890, the SAO moved to the grounds of the Harvard College Observatory in Cambridge, Massachusetts in the 1950s where

Independent

it documents new discoveries of comets, supernovae, and star outbursts. Its sister site is the **Harvard-Smithsonian Center for Astrophysics** at (http://sao-www.harvard.edu/cfa-home.html). Past issues of the **International Comet Quarterly** (http://sao-www.harvard.edu/cfa/ps/icq.html) are online.

Smithsonian Tropical Research Institute
http://www.si.edu/organiza/centers/stri/start.htm

Learn more about the tropics through photos and program descriptions. Topics include studies of animal behavior, canopy ecology, and molecular evolution.

Smithsonian Institution Libraries
http://www.si.edu/organiza/offices/silib/start.htm

Visit the branch archives, each devoted to a discipline. You'll find descriptions of their resources and databases online, as well as links to other Internet resources relating to their subjects.

Office of Elementary and Secondary Education
http://www.si.edu/organiza/offices/elemsec/start.htm

A *Smithsonian Resource Guide for Teachers* plus online curriculum guides and materials that teachers can download and use in classrooms.

Center for Folklife Programs and Cultural Studies
http://www.si.edu/organiza/offices/folklife/start.htm

The next best thing to visiting one of Smithsonian's favorite summer activities—the Festival of American Folklife on the Mall. Especially useful are the links to other Internet resources on American folklife.

Independent

Office of Printing and Photographic Services
http://www.si.edu/organiza/offices/photo/start.htm

Go to **Smithsonian Photographs Online** (http://photo2.si.edu) to access an array of exhibits that include documentation of the Million Man March, offerings left at the Vietnam Memorial Wall, a total eclipse of the moon, and aerial photos of the city of Washington.

The Smithsonian Associates
http://www.si.edu/youandsi/tsa/tsa.htm

Learn how you can support the museums and research through Smithsonian's various membership programs.

Smithsonian Affiliates

John F. Kennedy Center for the Performing Arts

Very little to do online at the Kennedy Center, but be sure to visit **ArtsEdge** (http://artsedge.kennedy-center.org), an online joint venture with the National Endowment for the Arts. Its goal is to link people, especially artists, teachers, and students, with information about the arts. The site features lots of conferences, contests, grants, and workshops. One fine example is the Young Artists Showcase. Be sure to visit the **Networks Users Guide,** where you'll find **The Web Spotlight,** a gateway to scores of sites for the arts education community. The **Search Lab** provides a database and collection of links and information on arts education, and the **Curriculum Studio** features arts-based K–12 materials.

The National Gallery of Art
http://www.si.edu/organiza/affil/natgal/start.htm

One of the finest collections in the world; illustrates Western European and American painting, sculpture, and graphic arts. At the time this

Independent

first edition was prepared, visitors could see highlights of the acclaimed Vermeer show. The individual galleries are not accessible here as they are in the other Smithsonian museums, but the exhibitions change more frequently and will be featured.

Woodrow Wilson International Center for Scholars
http://www.si.edu/organiza/affil/wilson/start.htm

Established to commemorate President Wilson's lifelong commitment to uniting scholarship with public affairs.

Smithsonian Resources

Now that we've completed our overview, we'll highlight a few other wonderful sites that are accessible through clickable icons on the Smithsonian home page.

Science in Cyberspace
http://www.si.edu/resource/science.htm

A joint effort of the Smithsonian and the National Science Foundation to produce electronic sites on the cutting edge of science research. Everything from fundamental principles to research in progress will be covered, with links to the best related sites throughout the world.

Discussion Groups
http://www.si.edu/resource/bbs.htm

As the name implies, an opportunity for cybervisitors to participate in ongoing discussions on a revolving set of topics posted at this site.

Smithsonian Magazine
http://www.smithsonianmag.si.edu

One of the great monthly magazines; back issues are available online.

Smithsonian Institution Research Information Service

http://www.si.edu/resource/library/start.htm

A computerized collection of research catalogs maintained by the Smithsonian's libraries and archives. Its four catalogs are: Libraries, Art Inventories (e.g., American Paintings Executed before 1914), Archives and Manuscripts, and Research/Bibliographies.

Planning a Visit

http://www.si.edu/welcome/planvis/start.htm

Advice for "real-time" visitors to the Mall in Washington—where to eat, where to stay, attractions for children, sightseeing, and other valuable tips.

People

http://www.si.edu/people/start.htm

Find out where to address questions about specific museums or subjects, how to contact the board and committees, and what jobs are currently available. Periodically, this site features "Meet Our Staff," a profile of a Smithsonian staffer.

Products

http://www.si.edu/products/start.htm

One of the pleasures of visiting any great museum is being able to stroll through the museum shop. Take your shopping cart and browse the displays of merchandise on sale at the **Smithsonian Mart** (150 of the most popular items from all the museums are tied into the 150th anniversary) and the **Smithsonian Shopping Mall.** Order by using the toll-free phone number. Two examples of what you can find in the Mart catalog: a reproduction of the Hope Diamond for $65, or, if you prefer to think cuddly, a Plush Panda for $36.

Independent

One last feature to know about. At **Perspectives** (http://www.si
.edu/perspect/start.htm) you'll find a potpourri of specific subjects
including Botany, Computers, Conservation, Dinosaurs, Gardens,
Mammals, Minerals and Gems, Reptiles, Textiles and Crafts; click on
any one of these for quick access to many of the treasures throughout
the Smithsonian web.

Best Sites for Business and Market Research

EDGAR (Securities and Exchange Commission)
(http://www.sec.gov/edgarhp.htm)

FRED (Federal Reserve)
(http://www.stls.frb.org/index.html)

GEMS (Global Export Market Information System)
(http://www.itaiep.doc.gov)

LOCIS (Library of Congress)
(http://lcweb.loc.gov/homepage/online.html)

Patent and Trademark Office
(http://www.uspto.gov)

Small Business Administration Hot Links
(http://www.sba.gov/hotlist)

State Department Commercial Guides and
Country Notes
(gopher://dosfan.lib.uic.edu/www/about_state
/about.html)

STAT-USA (Department of Commerce)
(http://www.stat-usa.gov)

TIGER Mapping Service (Census Bureau)
(http://tiger.census.gov)

The U.S. Business Advisor (White House)
(http://www.business.gov)

SOCIAL SECURITY ADMINISTRATION
http://www.ssa.gov

A broad, searchable site that answers almost any general question about Social Security, offers forms online, and shows you historical exhibits, statistics, and more. Much of the information is also offered in Spanish. The most useful source is the *Social Security Handbook.* The home page reminds you that questions on individual claims must be handled by phone, to preserve confidentiality. For further information, call (800) 772-1213.

Social Security Online Site Map
http://www.ssa.gov/sitemap.htm

An overview to the three dozen most useful sites at SSA.

Health Care Financing Administration
http://www.hcfa.gov

This agency administers Medicare and Medicaid, which together help pay medical bills for 70 million Americans. Get detailed information about eligibility, benefits, how to find additional insurance, how to cover gaps in service, and every other question you may have about the Medicare and Medicaid programs. If you work with a managed care program, look for a resource information directory online and FAQs about other types of health coverage plans.

Social Security Handbook
http://www.ssa.gov/OP_Home/handbook/ssa-hbk.htm

Everything you need to know about retirement, survivors, disability, supplemental security income (SSI), and health insurance. Use the index or table of contents to conduct your search.

Independent

Social Security Benefit Information

http://www.ssa.gov/programs/programs_intro.html

> Learn more about your Social Security status; includes a downloadable form for obtaining a replacement card.

The Pamphlet Rack

http://www.ssa.gov/programs/pamphlet_rack.html

> Easy access to the most requested publications, listed by category. The material is similar to the content of the *Handbook* (see above), but is far more accessible.

Office of Research and Statistics

http://www.ssa.gov/statistics/ors_home.html

> Your gateway to relevant data on the aging of America, which should be of special interest to researchers, academics, and trendwatchers.

Best Statistical Sources

Bureau of Justice Statistics
(http://www.ojp.usdoj.gov/bjs)

Bureau of Labor Statistics (http://stats.bls.gov)

Bureau of Transportation Statistics
(http://www.bts.gov)

Census Data Lookup
(http://www.census.gov/cdrom/lookup)

Federal Statistics Briefing Rooms
(http://www.whitehouse.gov/fsbr)

National Agricultural Statistics Service
(http://www.usda.gov/nass)

National Center for Health Statistics
(http://www.cdc.gov/nchswww/nchshome.htm)

NOAA's National Climatic Data Center
(http://www.ncdc.noaa.gov)

National Criminal Justice Research Service
(http://www.ncjrs.org)

NOAA's National Geophysical Data Center
(http://www.ngdc.noaa.gov)

NOAA's National Oceanographic Data Center
(http://www.nodc.noaa.gov)

Social Security Office of Research and Statistics
(http://www.ssa.gov/statistics/ors_home.html)

Statistical Abstract of the United States
(http://www.census.gov/stat_abstract)

Independent

TENNESSEE VALLEY AUTHORITY
http://www.tva.gov

Established in 1933, during the Great Depression, the TVA is now the largest public power producer in the country, and, as a by-product of its dams, manages 164 public recreation areas. The website offers a great deal of information about the agency—facts, vision, goals, press releases, and speeches by the chairman. Under "Using Shoreline Property or TVA Land," you can select a TVA-managed region and obtain an address and phone number to contact for more information.

Dare to Compare
http://www.tva.gov/dare/dare.htm

Use this interactive page to determine what your savings would be if you used an electric heat pump in place of a natural gas furnace.

For More Information
http://www.tva.gov/moreinfo/moreinfo.htm

More detailed descriptions of TVA resources, for example, "Buying Surplus Property from the TVA," "Doing Business with the TVA," and phone numbers for media inquiries and the TVA lake information line.

UNITED STATES AGENCY FOR INTERNATIONAL DEVELOPMENT
http://www.info.usaid.gov

> USAID conducts foreign assistance and humanitarian aid to advance the political and economic interests of the United States. Click on **Regional Information** to learn about aid programs throughout the world.

Bureau of Africa/Productive Sector Growth and Environment
http://www.usaid.gov/sdpsge/psgehome.html

> Learn of USAID's ongoing programs in Africa, from natural resources management to sustainable agricultural productivity and technology development and transfer.

Famine Early Warning System
http://www.info.usaid.gov/fews/fews.html

> Find out where food production and shortages are most threatening by reading monthly news bulletins and special reports.

Environmental and Energy Study Institute
http://www.info.usaid.gov/eesi/visual1.html

> Get the facts and figures on U.S. development assistance—how much is spent, where, and on what types of programs. The bar chart on the home page shows that 17 percent of the U.S. budget goes to national defense and 21 percent goes to Social Security (plus 14 percent to net interest), but only .5 percent goes to USAID. Dozens of bar graphs

Independent

illustrate mortality and fertility rates, food production, and the like. Especially grim was the graph at (http://www.info.usaid.gov/eesi/text /human/human2.html), which shows that the child mortality rate in seven African countries (e.g., Sierra Leone, Ethiopia, and Rwanda) is approximately 200 deaths per 1,000 children under age 5.

Demographic and Health Surveys
http://www.macroint.com/dhs

One of the world's largest primary sources of information on women and their families in Africa, Asia, Latin America, and the Caribbean. Since 1984, USAID has collaborated with developing country institutions to conduct surveys on fertility, family planning, child health, and household living conditions.

UNITED STATES HOLOCAUST MEMORIAL MUSEUM
http://www.ushmm.org

Although not reporting to any government agency, the U.S. Holocaust Memorial Council was established by Congress. The museum receives some federal funds (making it appropriate for inclusion in this book) but is dependent on private support. Since its opening in 1993, it has become one of the most visited museums on the Mall, and perhaps the most memorable. Its aim is to remember the Holocaust perpetrated in Europe by the Nazis in the 1930s and 1940s, but its exhibits are not limited to that period. The website offers several online exhibits via a keyword search through the archives data. Click on "Other Resources" to get a list of Holocaust organizations around the country and information on how to contact them.

Tickets are required to actually visit the Museum, and "Visiting the Museum" is an excellent previsit guide. An e-mail form allows you to make a group reservation online.

U.S. Holocaust Research Institute
http://www.ushmm.org/ri.html

The scholarly arm of the Museum gives details about the library and archive collections, plus an online finder's guide to the microfilmed documents collection (such as "Records of Nazi Concentration Camps, 1939–1945"). Learn about the photographic, oral history, film, and video archives (no examples are yet online), as well as The Benjamin and Vladka Meed Registry of Jewish Holocaust Survivors, which includes 100,000 records of survivors and their families. This site tells how to add a name(s) to the list.

Independent

Learning About the Holocaust

http://www.ushmm.org/holo.htm

Two remarkable teaching tools—"Guidelines for Teaching About the Holocaust" and "An Historical Summary"—can and should be downloaded here and used in classes and in the home.

UNITED STATES INFORMATION AGENCY
http://www.usia.gov

Created in 1948, USIA supports American foreign policy and promotes
the national interest through a range of overseas information programs.
The best known program is the J. William Fulbright Scholarships.
USIA sponsors the Voice of America radio network and maintains more
than 200 posts in 147 countries where it is known as USIS, the U.S.
Information Service.

Office of Research
http://www.usia.gov/usiahome/medreac.html

To be informed of overseas media reactions, read digests of the latest
editorial and op-ed pages in papers around the world regarding major
U.S. foreign policy issues. Sources range from *The Financial Times of
London* to *Izvestia* in Russia, *La Jornada* in Mexico, and *Liberation
Daily* in China.

Educational and Cultural Exchanges
http://www.usia.gov/educatio.html

Learn of the various programs that award grants to thousands of
American academics for lecturing or conducting research overseas.
The Fulbright Student Program provides grants to U.S. and foreign
students to study at the graduate level. The Hubert H. Humphrey
Fellowship Program brings mid-level professionals from developing
countries, Eastern and Central Europe, and the former Soviet Union to
the United States for a year of academic study. An excellent program
for nonacademics is the Artists as Ambassadors Program, which sends
gifted young American musicians to perform and work with musicians
overseas. For further information on all these programs and on the

Independent

USIA in general, including phone and fax numbers and mailing and e-mail addresses, click on **The Ties Which Unite Us** at this site.

Another useful site is the **Internet Resources for Student Advising** (http://www.usia.gov/education/advise.html), which provides links to the home pages of almost every American university as well as firms such as the Princeton Review and the Educational Testing Service.

Voice of America

http://www.voa.gov

One of the largest news-gathering organizations in the world, VOA is a lifeline of information about America, in 37 languages, to a worldwide overseas audience.

Best Interactive Tools for Consumer Information

Library of Congress LOCIS and Z39.50 Searches
(http://lcweb.loc.gov/homepage/online.html)

Representatives' e-mail addresses
(http://www.house.gov/Whoswho.html)

Senators' e-mail addresses
(http://www.senate.gov/senator/members.html)

Site Tree at IRS
(http://www.irs.ustreas.gov/prod/search/site_tree.html)

Thematic mapping system (Census Bureau)
(http://www.census.gov/themapit/www)

Box Score of Endangered Species (Fish and Wildlife Service)
(http://www.fws.gov/~r9endspp/boxscore.html)

U.S. Government Manual
(http://www.access.gpo/nara/nara001.html)

PLANTS Database (Department of Agriculture)
(http://plants.usda.gov:80/plants)

A number of the finest Internet tools in Uncle Sam's domain—for consumers and for businesses—are accessible only by subscription or prior registration. They include: **STAT-USA** (http://www.stat-usa.gov), a data-gathering tool at the Census Bureau, **CDC Wonder** (http://wonder.cdc.gov), a search engine at the Centers for Disease Control, **Internet Grateful Med** (http://igm.nlm.nih.gov), a search engine for MEDLINE and other data bases at the National Library of Medicine, and a daily news service from FedWorld called **World News Connection** (http://wnc.fedworld.gov) that draws upon thousands of foreign media sources—all translated into English. Consult the individual sites to see if and how you can apply for access.

Independent

UNITED STATES POSTAL SERVICE
http://www.usps.gov

A site you will likely return to on many occasions. Especially useful are the charts for retrieving zip codes and calculating proper postage for sending any kind of mail anywhere in the world. Stamp collectors will have a field day here.

Your Post Office
http://www.usps.gov/postofc/pstoffc.htm

Enter any address, and you'll have immediate access to its Zip+4 code.

Postage Rates
http://www.usps.gov/consumer/rates.htm

Find out the current postal fees for any kind of mail, from first class to bulk rate to international. Coming soon: a first class and priority mail postage calculator online.

Consumer Information
http://www.usps.gov/consumer

A FAQ may help you determine what happens to undeliverable mail. *The Consumer's Guide to the Postal Service* explains special mailing services (insurance, COD, and so on), how to mail to military posts, and other services like mail order and passport applications.

Stamps Center

http://www.usps.gov/postofc/stamps.htm

Get all of the latest stamp-related developments here, including pictures of the newest stamps and a pictorial record of all stamps released in the past few years.

Global ePOST

http://www.usps.gov/business/globalep.htm

A new service that delivers an electronic-to-hard volume mail service to several European countries and Australia. Global ePOST was inaugurated at the National Postal Forum in California on April 22, 1996 when the Xerox Corporation electronically sent 10,000 marketing letters for next day delivery by Deutsche Post AG, the national postal service of Germany.

Web Interactive Network of Government Services

http://www.wings.usps.gov/index.html

The post office, of all places, has designed one of the most creative web sites in Uncle Sam's domain. WINGS intends to be a one-stop information source for hundreds of consumer issues ranging from jobs to retirement. In fact, it features an innovative panel simply called *Life* which will offer direct access to Uncle Sam's websites that affect the lifecycle of birth, coming of age, marital status, retirement and death. Another panel, *Moving*, will display an online change of address form, among other features. Under construction when we visited, WINGS may be a regular stop for the denizens of cyberspace.

Independent

GLOSSARY OF WEB TERMINOLOGY

✯ ✯ ✯

✯ ✯ ✯

address *See* **URL.**

ARPAnet *Abbreviation for* **Advanced Research Projects Agency Network,** used originally by the Department of Defense. The network that later evolved into the Internet.

ASCII *Acronym for* **American Standard Code for Information Interchange.** The standard code that a computer uses to express letters, punctuation, and other characters. It can be understood by almost any computer running almost any operating system.

backbone The high-traffic, high-speed, high-density portion of any communications network. *Note:* On the Internet, the original backbone was the NSFnet.

binary A language computers use to transfer information using combinations of only two digits—1 and 0. *Note:* "BinHex" or "Binary Mode" is the common way that programs, pictures, and complex files are transferred over the Internet.

bit *Abbreviation for* **binary digit.** The smallest possible unit of computer information.

bits per second A measurement of how many bits can be transferred from one point to another in a single second. *Note:* Bits per second has surplanted baud as the unit of choice for measuring data transfer speeds.

browser   *Also* **web browser.** Any computer software program for reading hypertext, usually associated with the Internet and the World Wide Web. *Note:* A browser may be able to access information in many formats and through different protocols, including HTTP, FTP, and Gopher.

bulletin board system (BBS)   A computer system that is accessible by dialing a phone number and logging in using a modem and a computer. *Note:* For years, BBSes were the main source of online government information. They often are accessible now via the Internet and the World Wide Web.

byte   A sequence of adjacent bits (usually eight) which, when considered as a unit, represents a single character (a letter, or a symbol). Also used to measure the size of computer files. *Example:* The letter "F" is made up of one *byte,* the word "cat" is made up of three *bytes.*

clickable   An adjective describing a hypertext item found on a web page that the user can click on with a mouse to access specific information. *Note:* Something that is clickable can be text or an image. *Example:* A *clickable* map might allow the user to point and click on individual states to see them in higher relief.

database   A set of data required for a specific purpose or fundamental to a system, project, enterprise, or business. *Note:* Searchable databases are an essential tool of the World Wide Web. They allow users to find information by entering the subject, name, title, and so on, of whatever they are trying to find.

dial-up connection   A connection to a host computer in which a user initiates service using a modem over standard telephone lines. *Note:* Most home computer users connect to the Internet using a dial-up connection.

direct connection   A permanent (twenty-four-hour) connection between a computer and the Internet. *Note:* A direct connection is the Internet access method of choice for networks, institutions, and many businesses, but is more expensive because it requires leasing a special dedicated line from the telephone company.

domain name   The location name of a specific site somewhere on the Internet. *Note:* Domain names have two or more parts, separated by periods (dots), that tell the user more about them. The leftmost part of the name is the most specific; the part to the right is the most general. Domain names usually end in one of these suffixes: .edu (educational institution), .com (commercial), .gov (government), .mil (military), .org (nonprofit organization), or .net (network). *Examples:* http://www.loc.gov is the *domain name* for the Library of Congress Internet site, and http://www.whitehouse.gov is the *domain name* for The White House Internet site. *See also:* **URL.**

download   To transfer a copy of a computer file to the user's computer from another computer. *Note:* On the Internet, users will often have to download documents or files to their own computer before they can look at, listen to, see, or use them.

electronic forms   An electronic document with blanks to be filled in; commonly found on the World Wide Web. *Note:* An electronic form is much like its printed counterpart, but a user can send it electronically by pressing a button.

E-mail   An electronic means for communication in which text or data are transmitted and held in storage until called for by the addressee.

FAQ   *Abbreviation for* **Frequently Asked Questions.** An online file that answers frequently asked questions, thereby assisting new users and avoiding repetitive offline inquiries.

FTP   *Abbreviation for* **File Transfer Protocol.** A method that allows computers connected to the Internet to transfer files between them. *Note:* Connecting to a site on the Internet via FTP is a good way to access depositories of documents, files, and other downloadable information.

gopher   A menu-based information-searching tool that allows users to access various types of databases, such as FTP archives and white pages databases; a precursor to the World Wide Web browser. *Note:* Gopher sites are also accessible with a web browser. They can be identified by the word "gopher" at the beginning of the URL (instead of "http" or "ftp").

homepage   The first document encountered at a website; usually includes information on how to access different parts of the site. *Note:* A good analogy for a home page is the cover and table of contents of a book.

HTML   *Abbreviation for* **Hypertext Markup Language.** A language used to write web pages. Allows the use of hypertext, and formats the presentation of the page.

HTTP   *Abbreviation for* **Hypertext Transfer Protocol.** In the World Wide Web, the method used to transfer hypertext-based files from one computer to another over the Internet.

hyperlink   *Also* **hypertext link** or **link.** The connections (appearing on the screen as hypertext) that allow the user to follow references to different parts of the World Wide Web. *Example:* The White House has *hyperlinks* to each of the executive agencies. A user can follow them by clicking on hypertext that reads "Commerce Department" or "Department of Defense." The web browser will move to those websites automatically, without requiring the user to type in an address.

hypertext   On the screen of a web page, text that is often underlined or in some color distinguishing it from standard type. When clicked on, it instructs the web browser to move to a different location on the World Wide Web.

Internet   The worldwide interconnection of individual networks operated by government, industry, academia, and private parties. Many people use internet and world wide web interchangably, but in fact the world wide web is a subset of the internet. *Note:* The Internet originally served to interconnect laboratories engaged in government research, and has now been expanded to serve millions of users and a multitude of purposes.

internet   Any interconnection of networks.

kilobyte   Literally, 1,000 bytes. A common unit used to measure the size of computer files. *Note:* Before downloading a file off of the Internet, it is often useful to see how large it is, in kilobytes or megabytes, in order to gauge the amount of time it will take to download.

link   *See* **hyperlink.**

login/logon   The procedure that is followed by a user in beginning a computer session.

lynx   A text-based web browser, popular for people with slow connections.

megabyte   Literally, 1 million bytes. A common unit used to measure the size of computer files. *Note:* Before downloading a file off of the Internet, it is often useful to see how large it is, in kilobytes or megabytes, in order to gauge the amount of time it will take to download.

modem   *Acronym for* **modulator/demodulator.** A device used to connect one computer to another over regular telephone lines. *Note:* A modem at one end converts digital signals into analog signals suitable for transmission over regular telephone lines; another modem at the other end of the phone line translates the analog signals back into digital signals that the computer can understand.

Mosaic   One of the first web browsers; provides a graphical user interface for reading and using web pages.

network   Any connection of two or more computers that are able to "talk" to each other.

Netscape   A popular web browser that provides a graphical user interface for reading and using web pages.

node   Any single computer attached to a network.

NSFnet   *Acronym for* **National Science Foundation Network.** The network, created in the mid-1980s, that was the original backbone of the Internet.

public domain   The status of any material that is not copyrighted and can be freely copied and distributed.

search engine   An Internet tool that searches a database or other collection of information on the basis of keywords set by the user. *Note:* Some search engines (often found on a homepage) allow the user to search all of the content in a website. Others allow the user to search the contents of a specific database of information.

server   A network device that manages the shared resources of the network. *Example:* A web *server* manages the web pages of a network by directing communications and splitting chores among different computers.

service provider   A company that provides access, either by dial-up or direct connection, to the Internet or other online service.

TCP/IP   *Abbreviation for* **Transmission Control Protocol/ Internet Protocol.** The standard communications protocol originally developed by the U.S. Department of Defense; allows computers of different types to "talk" to each other over the Internet.

telnet   A program that allows users to give commands to another computer on the Internet as if it were their own computer. *Note:* The word "telnet" sometimes appears at the beginning of a web address. When the address is accessed from a web browser, in most cases a window to a "telnet site" opens automatically, and a user accesses the telnet site by logging in at this window.

URL *Acronym for* **Universal Resource Locator.** The complete command that, when entered into a web browser, allows a user to access any site that is a part of the World Wide Web. *Example:* The full *URL* for the Department of Energy is http://www.doe.gov, where the "http://" tells the user that the address uses the Hypertext Transport Protocol, or, in English, that it is a web page. telnet://vaonline.va.gov is the *URL* for the Department of Veterans Affairs telnet site. The "telnet://" marks it as a telnet site instead of a web page, and thus a telnet window appears when this *URL* is entered. *See also:* **domain name, FTP, gopher, HTTP, telnet.**

web browser *See* **browser.**

web page Any individual location on a website that was written in html. *Note:* A web page can be all text, combine images and text, or be made up completely of hypertext (clickable) images.

website Any location on the Internet that is part of the World Wide Web. Also, a collection of web pages that appear together under the same domain.

World Wide Web An international network-based information service composed of Internet host computers that provide online information in a hypertext format. *Note:* Information on the World Wide Web is accessed with a hypertext browser such as Mosaic or Netscape. The essence of its usefulness is that there is no hierarchy of information, and the same information may be found by many different approaches (thus, a "web").

Alphabetical Listing
of Websites

Aberdeen Test Center
    (http://dale.apg.army.mil)
A Biologist's Guide to the Internet
    (http://www.nfrcg.gov/home-page/htmls.html)
About the National Archives
    (http://gopher.nara.gov:70/1/about)
A Career Planning Center
    (http://www2.nas.edu/cpc/index.html)
Access EPA
    (http://www.epa.gov/Access)
ACQ Web
    (http://www.acq.osd.mil)
A Day in the Life of a President
    (http://www2.sils.umich.edu/FordLibrary/DayInTheLife.html)
Administration on Aging
    (http://www.aoa.dhhs.gov/aoa/index.html)
Administration for Children and Families
    (http://www.acf.dhhs.gov)
Administrative Office of the United States Courts
    (http://www.uscourts.gov)
Adult, Career and Vocational Education (ERIC)
    (http://www.acs.ohio-state.edu/units/education/cete/ericacve/index.html)
Advanced Research Projects Agency
    (http://www.arpa.mil)
Advanced Technology Program
    (http://www.atp.nist.gov)
African-American Mosaic, The
    (http://lcweb.loc.gov/exhibits/african/intro.html)
Age Pages, The
    (http://www.aoa.dhhs.gov/aoa/pages/info.html/#agepage)
Agricultural Marketing Service
    (http://www.usda.gov/ams/titlepag.htm)
AIDS Clinical Trials Information Service
    (http://www.actis.org)
AIDS Patent Project
    (http://app.cnidr.org)
Air Combat Command
    (http://www.acc.af.mil)
Air Combat Command map
    (http://www.acc.af.mil/acc_sites.html)
Air Education and Training Command
    (http://www.aetc.af.mil)
Air Education and Training Command map
    (http://www.aetc.af.mil/AETC-Bases)
Air Force Link
    (http://www.dtic.dla.mil/airforcelink/index.html)

Air Force Materiel Command
(http://www.afmc.wpafb.af.mil:12000)
Air Force Reserves
(http://www.afres.af.mil)
Air Force Sites
(http://www.dtic.mil/airforcelink/sites/)
Airman (Air Force)
(http://www.dtic.dla.mil/airforcelink/pa/airman/cover.htm)
Air Mobility Command
(http://www.safb.af.mil/hqamc/pa)
Air Traffic Controller Academy
(http://www.ama500.jccbi.gov)
Air Weather Service
(http://infosphere.safb.af.mil/users/aws/public_www)
Alternative Fuels Data Center
(http://www.afdc.doe.gov)
Altus AFB, OK
(http://www.lts.aetc.af.mil)
Amazing Facts (NASA)
(http://pao.gsfc.nasa.gov/gsfc/earth/efacts/efacts.htm)
American Folklife Center
(http://lcweb.loc.gov/folklife)
American Memory (Library of Congress)
(http://lcweb2.loc.gov/amhome.html)
America's Job Bank
(http://www.ajb.dni.us)
America's Labor Market Information System
(http://ecuvax.cis.ecu.edu/~lmi/lmi.html)
Ames Research Center
(http://www.arc.nasa.gov)
Anacostia Museum
(http://www.si.edu/organiza/museums/anacost/start.htm)
Andersen AFB, Guam
(http://www.andersen.af.mil)
Animal and Plant Health Inspection Service
(http://www.aphis.usda.gov)
Antitrust Division (DOJ)
(http://gopher.usdoj.gov/atr/atr.htm)
Apollo 11
(http://www.nasa.gov/hqpao/apollo_11.html)
Apollo Manned Space Program
(http://www.nasm.edu:80/APOLLO/Apollo.html)
Applying for Grants (Education Department)
(http://www.ed.gov/pubs/KnowAbtGrants)
Archeology
(http://www.cr.nps.gov/archeo.html)
Archives of American Art
(http://www.si.edu/organiza/offices/archart/start.htm)
A Researcher's Guide to the Department of Education
(http://www.ed.gov/pubs/ResearchersGuide)
Argonne National Laboratory
(http://www.anl.gov)
Army Alumni Organizations
(http://www.army.mil/vetinfo/vetloc.htm)
Army/Library of Congress Country Studies
(http://lcweb.loc.gov/homepage/country.html)
Armylink
(http://www.army.mil)
Army Recruiting
(http://www.usarec.army.mil)

Army Research Laboratory
  (http://info.arl.army. mil)
Army Retirement Services
  (http://www.army.mil/retire-p/retire.htm)
Army ROTC
  (http://www-tradoc.army.mil/rotc/index.html)
Arnold AFB, TN
  (http://info.arnold.af.mil)
Arthur M. Sackler Gallery
  (http://www.si.edu/organiza/museums/artsack/start.htm)
Arts and Industries Building
  (http://www.si.edu/organiza/museums/artsind/start.htm)
Asia-Pacific Technology Program
  (http://www.doc.gov/aptp.html)
AskERIC Virtual Library
  (http://ericir.syr.edu)
Assessment and Evaluation (ERIC)
  (http://www.cua.edu/www/eric_ae)
Asteroid and Comet Impact Hazard
  (http://ccf.arc.nasa.gov/sst)
  (http://george.arc.nasa.gov/sst)
Astronaut Biographies
  (http://www.jsc.nasa.gov/Bios/astrobio.html)
A Teacher's Guide to the Department of Education
  (http://www.ed.gov/pubs/TeachersGuide)
Atlas of Mars
  (http://fi-www.arc.nasa.gov/fia/projects/bayes-group/Atlas/Mars)
Aviation Weather Center
  (http://www.awc-kc.noaa.gov)
Aviano AB, Italy
  (http://www.avi.af.mil)
A Walk Through Time (NIST)
  (http://physics.nist.gov/GenInt/Time/time.html)

Barksdale AFB
  (http://bncc-w3.barksdale.af.mil)
Basics of Space Flight Learners' Workbook
  (http://www.jpl.nasa.gov/basics)
Beale AFB
  (http://www.beale.af.mil)
BEMS (Big Emerging Markets)
  (http://www.stat-usa.gov/itabems.html)
Bosnia Link
  (http://www.dtic.mil/bosnia/army)
Box Score of Endangered Species (Fish and Wildlife Service)
  (http://www.fws.gov/~r9endspp/boxscore.html)
Brief Guides to the Internet
  (http://lcweb.loc.gov/loc/guides)
Briefing Room, The
  (http://www.whitehouse.gov/WH/html/briefroom.html)
Brookhaven National Laboratory
  (http://suntid.bnl.gov:8080/bnl.html)
Brooks AFB, TX
  (http://www.brooks.af.mil)
Bureau of Africa/Productive Sector Growth and Environment
  (http://www.usaid.gov/sdpsge/psgehome.html)
Bureau of Alcohol, Tobacco, and Firearms
  (http://www.ustreas.gov/treasury/bureaus/atf/atf.html)
Bureau of Consular Affairs/Travel Information
  (http://travel.state.gov)

Bureau of Consular Information (State)
(http://travel.state.gov)
Bureau of Economic Analysis
(http://www.bea.doc.gov)
Bureau of Indian Affairs
(http://info.er.usgs.gov/doi/bureau-indian-affairs.html)
Bureau of Justice Statistics
(http://www.ojp.usdoj.gov/bjs)
Bureau of Labor Statistics
(http://stats.bls.gov)
Bureau of Labor Statistics Regional Information
(http://stats.bls.gov:80/regnhome.htm)
Bureau of Land Management
(http://www.blm.gov)
Bureau of Transportation Statistics
(http://www.bts.gov)
Buying a Home
(http://www.hud.gov/buying.html)

Cannon AFB
(http://ns2.cannon.af.mil)
Career Planning Center (National Academy of Sciences)
(http://www2.nas.edu/cpc/index.html)
Carl Hayden Bee Research Center, The
(http://gears.tucson.ars.ag.gov)
Cascades Volcano Observatory
(http://vulcan.wr.usgs.gov)
Cassini Spacecraft Movies
(http://www.jpl.nasa.gov/cassini/Movies/index.html)
Catalog of Federal Domestic Assistance
(http://www.gsa.gov/fdac)
Catalogue of Federal Domestic Assistance
(http://www.ed.gov/programs.html#CFDA)
CDC Prevention Guidelines Database
(http://wonder.cdc.gov/wonder/prevguid/prevguid.htm)
CDC Wonder
(http://wonder.cdc.gov)
Census Bureau
(http://www.census.gov)
Census Bureau Data Maps
(http://www.census.gov/statab/www/profile.html)
Census Data Lookup
(http://www.census.gov/cdrom/lookup)
Census State Data Centers
(http://www.census.gov/sdc/www)
Center for Analysis and Prediction of Storms
(http://wwwcaps.uoknor.edu)
Center for Army Lessons Learned
(http://call.army.mil:1100/call.html)
Center for Computer Graphics and Scientific Visualization
(http://www.cs.brown.edu/stc)
Center for Drug Evaluation and Research
(gopher://gopher.cder.fda.gov)
Center for Earth and Planetary Studies
(http://ceps.nasm.edu:2020/homepage.html)
Center for Folklife Programs and Cultural Studies
(http://www.si.edu/organiza/offices/folklife/start.htm)
Center for Food Safety
(http://vm.cfsan.fda.gov/list.html)
Center for Mars Exploration
(http://cmex-www.arc.nasa.gov)

Center of Military History (Army)
    (http://imabbs.army.mil/cmh-pg/default.htm)
Center for Particle Astrophysics
    (http://physics7.berkeley.edu/home.html)
Center for Research in Cognitive Science
    (http://www.cis.upenn.edu/~ircs/homepage.html)
Center for Research on Parallel Computation
    (http://www.crpc.rice.edu/CRPC)
Center for Superconductivity
    (http://www.stcs.uiuc.edu)
Center for Urban Ecology
    (http://www.nbs.gov/nbs2/cuehome)
Center for Veterinary Medicine
    (http://www.cvm.fda.gov)
Centers for Disease Control
    (http://www.cdc.gov)
Central Intelligence Agency
    (http://www.odci.gov/cia)
Charters of Freedom (National Archives)
    (http://www.nara.gov/exhall/charters/charters.html)
Chips (Navy)
    (http://www.chips.navy.mil/chips)
CIA Publications
    (http://www.odci.gov/cia/publications/pubs.html)
CIA World Factbook
    (http://www.odci.gov/cia/publications/95fact/index.html)
CIC's Most Popular Publications, The
    (http://www.pueblo.gsa.gov/top20.htm)
Civil Air Patrol
    (http://www.cap.af.mil)
Civil Division (DOJ)
    (http://gopher.usdoj.gov/civil/civil.html)
Civil Rights Division (DOJ)
    (http://gopher.usdoj.gov/crt/crt-home.html)
Civil War Battlefields (National Park Service)
    (http://www.cr.nps.gov/abpp/battles/Contents.html)
Civil War Soldiers and Sailors System
    (http://www.cr.nps.gov/itd/welcome.html)
Climate Prediction Center
    (http://nic.fb4.noaa.gov)
Coast Guard Auxiliary
    (http://131.230.57.1)
Coastal Ecosystems
    (http://www.fws.gov/~cep/cepcode.html)
CodeTalk for Native Americans
    (http://www.codetalk.fed.us)
Columbus AFB
    (http://www.col.aetc.af.mil)
Comet Observation
    (http://encke.jpl.nasa.gov)
Comet Shoemaker-Levy
    (http://www.jpl.nasa.gov/sl9)
Command and General Staff College
    (http://www-cgsc.army.mil)
Commercial Technology Electronic Network
    (http://ctoserver.arc.nasa.gov)
Community Center (DHUD)
    (http://www.hud.gov/communit.html)
Community Colleges (ERIC)
    (http://www.gse.ucla.edu/ERIC/eric.html)

Congressional Special Services Office
(http://www.senate.gov/tour/csso.html)
Consumer Alert! Online Scams (FTC)
(http://www.ftc.gov/bcp/scams01.htm)
Consumer Complaints Database (NHTSA)
(http://www.nhtsa.dot.gov/nsa/nsasearch.shtml)
Consumer Information (USPS)
(http://www.usps.gov/consumer)
Consumer Information Center
(http://www.pueblo.gsa.gov)
Consumer Line (FTC)
(http://www.ftc.gov/bcp/conline/conline.htm)
(consumerline@ftc.gov)
Consumer Product Safety Commission
(http://www.cpsc.gov)
(info@cpsc.gov)
Cooper-Hewitt National Design Museum
(http://www.si.edu/organiza/museums/design/start.htm)
Copyright Application Forms
(http://lcweb.loc.gov/copyright/forms.html)
Corporation for National Service, The
(http://www1.whitehouse.gov/WH/EOP/cns/html/cns-index.html)
Corporation for Public Broadcasting
(http://www.cpb.org)
Council on Environmental Quality
(http://ceq.eh.doe.gov)
Counseling and Student Services (ERIC)
(http://www.uncg.edu:80/~ericcas2)
Countries Where Peace Corps Volunteers Serve
(http://www.peacecorps.gov/www/io/country1.html)
Country Studies and Area Handbooks (LOC)
(http://lcweb.loc.gov/homepage/country.html)
Criminal Division (DOJ)
(http://gopher.usdoj.gov/criminal/criminal-home.html)
C-SPAN
(http://www.c-span.org)

Dante II
(http://maas-neotek.arc.nasa.gov/dante)
Dante II Mission Images
(http://img.arc.nasa.gov/Dante/images.html)
Dare to Compare (TVA)
(http://www.tva.gov/dare/dare.htm)
Davis-Monthan AFB
(http://www.dm.af.mil)
D.C. Circuit (U.S. Court of Appeals)
(http://www.ll.georgetown.edu/Fed-Ct/cadc.html)
Declaring Independence: Drafting the Documents
(http://lcweb.loc.gov/exhibits/declara/declara1.html)
Defense Acquisition Information
(http://www.dtic.dla.mil/hovlane)
Defense Reutilization and Marketing Service
(http://www.drms.dla.mil)
Defense Technical Information Service
(http://www.dtic.mil)
Demographic and Health Surveys
(http://www.macroint.com/dhs)
Department of Agriculture
(http://www.usda.gov)
Department of Commerce
(http://www.doc.gov)

Department of Commerce GLOBUS
      (http://www.stat-usa.gov/BEN/Services/globus.html)
Department of Defense
      (http://www.dtic.dla.mil/defenselink)
Department of Defense Fact File, The
      (http://www.dtic.dla.mil/defenselink/factfile)
Department of Education
      (http://www.ed.gov)
Department of Energy
      (http://www.doe.gov)
Department of Energy 1-800 Information Lines
      (http://www.hr.doe.gov/800numb.html)
Department of Energy Procurement Homepage
      (http://www.doe.gov/procure/prpages.html)
Department of Energy Research Labs
      (http://www.doe.gov/html/doe/infolink/usdoemap.html)
Department of Engraving and Printing
      (http://www.ustreas.gov:802/treasury/bureaus/bep/bep.html)
Department of Health and Human Services
      (http://www.os.dhhs.gov)
Department of Housing and Urban Development
      (http://www.hud.gov)
Department of the Interior
      (http://www.doi.gov)
Department of Justice
      (http://www.usdoj.gov)
Department of Labor
      (http://www.dol.gov)
Department of the Navy
      (http://www.navy.mil)
Department of Space History
      (http://www.nasm.edu/NASMDOCS/DEPT_SH.html)
Department of State
      (http://www.state.gov)
Department of State Gopher
      (gopher://dosfan.lib.uic.edu)
Department of Transportation
      (http://www.dot.gov)
Department of the Treasury
      (http://www.ustreas.gov)
Department of Veterans Affairs
      (http://www.va.gov)
Digital Classroom, The
      (http://www.nara.gov/nara/digital/classroom.html)
Digital Library Collections
      (http://lcweb.loc.gov/homepage/digital.html)
Direct Loan Program (Department of Education)
      (http://www.ed.gov/offices/OPE/DirectLoan)
Directorate for Education and Human Resources (NSF)
      (http://red.www.nsf.gov)
Directory of Senators
      by name: (http://www.senate.gov/senator/members.html)
      by state: (http://www.senate.gov/senator/state.html)
Disabilities and Gifted Education (ERIC)
      (gopher://ericir.syr.edu:70/11/Clearinghouses/16houses/ERIC_EC)
Disaster Application Center
      (http://www.fema.gov/fema/dac.html)
Discussion Groups (Smithsonian)
      (http://www.si.edu/resource/bbs.htm)
Division of Energy and Mineral Resources (BIA)
      (http://snake2.cr.usgs.gov)

DOC contents page
    (http://www.doc.gov/agencies.html)
DOD Education Gateway
    (http://www.acq.osd.mil/ddre/edugate)
DOD Laboratories
    (http://www.dtic.dla.mil/labman/projects/list.html)
Drug Enforcement Administration (DOJ)
    (http://www.usdoj.gov/dea/deahome.htm)
Dryden Flight Research Center
    (http://www.dfrc.nasa.gov/dryden.html)
Dwight D. Eisenhower Library
    (http://sunsite.unc.edu/lia/president/eisenhower.html)
Dyess AFB
    (http://www.dyess.af.mil)

Earth Science Information Center
    (http://www-nmd.usgs.gov/esic/esic.html)
EDGAR Database (Securities and Exchange Commission)
    (http://www.sec.gov/edgarhp.htm)
ED Supported Sites
    (http://www.ed.gov/EdRes/EdFed/OtherED.html)
Educational and Cultural Exchanges
    (http://www.usia.gov/educatio.html)
Educational Management (ERIC)
    (http://darkwing.uoregon.edu/,ericcem/home.html)
Educational Resources (House of Representatives)
    (http://www.house.gov/Educat.html)
Educational Resources (USGS)
    (http://www-nmd.usgs.gov/www/html/1educate.html)
Edwards AFB, CA
    (http://www.elan.af.mil)
Eglin AFB, FL
    (http://www.eglin.af.mil)
Eielson AFB, AK
    (http://icebox.eielson.af.mil)
Eighth Circuit (U.S. Court of Appeals)
    (http://www.wulaw.wustl.edu/8th.cir)
Einsiedlerhof AS, Germany Warrior Preparation Center
    (http://www.wpc.af.mil)
Eisenhower National Clearinghouse for Mathematics and Science Education
    (http://www.enc.org)
Eldercare Locator, The
    (http://www.aoa.dhhs.gov/aoa/pages/loctrnew.html)
Electronic Commerce Resource Sites (FinanceNet)
    (http://www.financnet.gov/ec.htm)
Electronic Services (IRS)
    (http://www.irs.ustreas.gov/prod/elec_svs/index.html)
Electronic Smithsonian
    (http://www.si.edu/electrsi/start.htm)
Electronic Texts and Publishing Resources
    (http://lcweb.loc.gov/global/etext)
Electronic Visitor Center, The (NPS)
    (http://www.nps.gov/facts.html)
Elementary and Early Childhood Education (ERIC)
    (http://ericps.ed.uiuc.edu/ericeece.html)
Eleventh Circuit (U.S. Court of Appeals)
    (http://www.law.emory.edu/11circuit)
Ellsworth AFB
    (http://www.ellsworth.af.mil)
Elmendorf AFB, AK
    (http://www.topcover.af.mil)

El Niño Theme Page
(http://www.pmel.noaa.gov/toga-tao/el-nino)
Employment and Training Administration
(http://www.doleta.gov)
Encyclopedia, The (Smithsonian)
(http://www.si.edu/welcome/faq/start.htm)
Endangered Species Bulletin map
(http://www.fws.gov/~r9endspp/stat-reg.html)
Endangered Species Program
(http://www.fws.gov/~r9endspp/endspp.html)
Energy Efficiency Clearinghouse and Renewable Energy Network
(http://www.nrel.gov/documents/erec_fact_sheets/erec.html)
Energy Efficiency and Renewable Energy Network
(http://www.eren.doe.gov)
Energy Information Administration
(http://www.eia.doe.gov)
ENIAC
(http://ftp.arl.mil/~mike/comphist)
Environmental and Energy Study Institute
(http://www.info.usaid.gov/eesi/visual1.html)
Environmental Protection Agency
(http://www.epa.gov)
Environmental Protection Agency Contracts
(http://www.epa.gov/epahome/Contracts.html)
Environmental Research Laboratories
(http://www.erl.noaa.gov)
Environment and Natural Resources Division (DOJ)
(http://gopher.usdoj.gov/enrd/enrd-home.html)
EPA Publications
(http://www.epa.gov/epahome/publications.html)
ERIC Document Reproduction Service
(http://edrs.com)
ERIC: Educational Resources Information Center
(http://www.aspensys.com/eric)
Ernest Orlando Lawrence Berkeley National Laboratory
(http://www.lbl.gov)
Ethnographic Studies
(http://lcweb.loc.gov/folklife/other.html)
Executive Office of the President
(http://www.whitehouse.gov/WH/EOP/html/couples.html)
Expanding Your Business
(http://www.sba.gov/business_expansion/ExpandingYourBusiness.html)
Expendable Launch Vehicle Program (JFK Space Center)
(http://www.ksc.nasa.gov/elv/elvpage.htm)
Exploration in Education
(http://stsci.edu/exined-html/exined-home.html)
Export-Import Bank, The
(http://www.exim.gov)
EZ/EC Community Toolbox
(http://www.ezec.gov/toolbox/guide/et/et.html)
EZ/EC—The Empowerment Zone and Enterprise Community Program
(http://www.ezec.gov)

FAFSA Express
(http://www.ed.gov/offices/OPE/express.html)
Famine Early Warning System
(http://www.info.usaid.gov/fews/fews.html)
Farm Service Agency
(http://www.fsa.usda.gov)
Federal Acquisition Jumpstation
(http://procure.msfc.nasa.gov/fedproc/home.html)

Federal Aviation Administration
    (http://www.faa.gov)
Federal Bureau of Investigation
    (http://www.fbi.gov)
Federal Bureau of Prisons
    (http://www.usdoj.gov/bop/bop.html)
Federal Circuit (U.S. Court of Appeals)
    (http://www.ll.georgetown.edu/Fed-Ct/cafed.html)
Federal Communications Commission
    (http://www.fcc.gov)
Federal Deposit Insurance Corporation
    (http://www.fdic.gov)
Federal Emergency Management Agency
    (http://www.fema.gov)
Federal Information Center
    (http://www.gsa.gov:80/et/fic-firs/fichome.htm)
Federal Information Exchange
    (http://web.fie.com)
Federal Job Announcement Search
    (http://www.fedworld.gov/jobs/jobsearch.html)
Federal Judicial Center
    (http://www.fjc.gov)
Federal Register
    (gopher//gopher.nara.gov:70/11/register/toc)
Federal Reserve Bank of Atlanta
    (http://www.frbatlanta.org)
Federal Reserve Bank of Boston
    (http://www.bos.frb.org)
Federal Reserve Bank of Chicago
    (http://www.frbchi.org)
Federal Reserve Bank of Cleveland
    (http://www.clev.frb.org)
Federal Reserve Bank of Dallas
    (http://www.dallasfed.org)
Federal Reserve Bank of Minneapolis
    (http://woodrow.mpls.frb.fed.us)
Federal Reserve Bank of New York
    (http://www.ny.frb.org)
Federal Reserve Bank of Philadelphia
    (http://www.libertynet.org/~fedresrv/fedpage.html)
Federal Reserve Bank of St. Louis
    (http://www.stls.frb.org)
Federal Reserve Bank of San Francisco
    (http://www.frbsf.org)
Federal Reserve System
    (http://www.clev.frb.org/fedlinks.htm)
Federal Statistics Briefing Rooms
    (http://www.whitehouse.gov/fsbr)
Federal Trade Commission
    (http://www.ftc.gov)
Federal Transit Administration
    (http://www.fta.dot.gov)
FedWorld
    (http://www.fedworld.gov)
FEMA's Help After A Disaster Page
    (http://www.fema.gov/fema/help.html)
Fermi National Accelerator Laboratory
    (http://www.fnal.gov)
Fifth Circuit (U.S. Court of Appeals)
    (http://www.law.utexas.edu/us5th/us5th.html)

FinanceNet
  (http://www.financenet.gov)
Financing Your Business
  (http://www.sba.gov/business_finances/FinancingYourBusiness.html)
First Circuit (U.S. Court of Appeals)
  (http://www.law.emory.edu/1circuit)
Fleet Numerical Meteorology andOceanography Center, The
  (http://metoc.fnoc.navy.mil)
Food Assistance Programs
  (http://www.usda.gov/fcs/fcsinfo.htm)
Food and Consumer Service
  (http://www.usda.gov/fcs/fcs.htm)
Food and Drug Administration
  (http://www.fda.gov)
Food Labeling
  (http://vm.cfsan.fda.gov/label.html)
Food and Nutrition Information Center
  (http://www.nalusda.gov/fnic)
Foreign Agricultural Service
  (http://www.usda.gov/fas)
Foreign Newspapers
  (http://lcweb.loc.gov/global/ncp/oltitles.html)
Forest Service
  (http://www.fs.fed.us)
Forest Service map
  (http://www.fs.fed.us/recreation/map.htm)
Forest Service reservations
  (http://www.fs.fed.us/recreation/campres.htm)
For More Information (TVA)
  (http://www.tva.gov/moreinfo/moreinfo.htm)
Fort Benning
  (http://www.benning.army.mil)
Fort Bliss
  (http://bliss-www.army.mil)
Fort Bragg
  (http://www.bragg.army.mil)
Fort Campbell
  (http://campbell-emh5.army.mil/campbell.htm)
Fort Carson
  (http://www.carson.army.mil)
Fort Detrick
  (http://www.medcom.amedd.army.mil/detrick)
Fort Eustis
  (http://www.eustis.army.mil)
Fort Gordon
  (http://www.gordon.army.mil)
Fort Hood
  (http://www.hood-pao.army.mil)
Fort Huachuca
  (http://huachuca-usaic.army.mil)
Fort Jackson
  (http://jackson-www.army.mil)
Fort Knox
  (http://147.238.100.101)
Fort Leavenworth
  (http://www-cgsc.army.mil)
Fort Lee
  (http://cascom-www.army.mil)
Fort Leonard Wood
  (http://www.wood.army.mil)

Fort McClellan
        (http://www-tradoc.army.mil/mcclellan)
Fort McCoy-Chapel
        (http://www.msilbaugh.com/mchapel.htm)
Fort McPherson
        (http://www.mcphersn.army.mil)
Fort Meade
        (http://www.mdw.army.mil/meade.htm)
Fort Monmouth
        (http://www.monmouth.army.mil)
Fort Monroe
        (http://www-tradoc.monroe.army.mil/monroe)
Fort Stewart and Hunter Army Airfield
        (http://158.20.22.136)
Fort Wainwright
        (http://143.213.12.254/home.htm)
Fourth Circuit (U.S. Court of Appeals)
        (http://www.law.emory.edu/4circuit)
Franklin D. Roosevelt Library
        (http://www.academic.marist.edu/fdr/fdrintro.htm)
FRED (Federal Reserve)
        (http://www.stls.frb.org/index.html)
Freer Gallery of Art, The
        (http://www.si.edu/organiza/museums/freer/start.htm)

Galileo Probe
        (http://ccf.arc.nasa.gov/galileo_probe)
Genealogy
        (http://clio.nara.gov:70/genealog)
Genealogy Information
        (http://www.census.gov/genealogy/www)
        (gopher://gopher.nara.gov:70/11/genealog)
General Accounting Office
        (http://www.gao.gov)
General Services Administration
        (http://www.gsa.gov)
General Services Administration Electronic Commerce Program Management Office
        (http://www.gsa.gov/ecapmo)
Geological and Geophysical Research
        (http://geology.usgs.gov)
George Bush Presidential Materials Project
        (http://csdl.tamu.edu/bushlib/bushpage.html)
George C. Marshall Space Flight Center
        (http://www.msfc.nasa.gov)
George Washington and Thomas Jefferson
        (http://lcweb2.loc.gov:8081/ammem/GW)
Gerald R. Ford Library/Museum
        (http://sunsite.unc.edu/lia/president/ford.html)
Gettysburg Address
        (http://lcweb.loc.gov/exhibits/G.Address/ga.html)
GILS (EPA)
        (http://www.epa.gov/gils)
Global Emergency Management System
        (http://www.fema.gov/fema/gems.html)
Global ePOST
        (http://www.usps.gov/business/globalep.htm)
Global Export Market Information System
        (http://www.itaiep.doc.gov)
Global Legal Information Network
        (http://lcweb2.loc.gov/glin/glinhome.html)

GLOBE Program (Global Learning and Observations to Benefit the Environment)
(http://www.globe.gov)
GLOBE Program for Kids, The
(http://globe.fsl.noaa.gov)
Go Army!
(http://www.usma.edu/BeatNavy.html)
Goddard Institute for Space Studies
(http://www.giss.nasa.gov)
Goddard Space Flight Center
(http://pao.gsfc.nasa.gov/gsfc.html)
Goodfellow AFB, TX
(http://www.gdf.aetc.af.mil)
Government Contracting (SBA)
(http://www.sba.gov/gopher/Government-Contracting)
Government Information Locator Service
(http://www.access.gpo.gov/su_docs/gils/gils.html)
(http://info.er.usgs.gov/gils/index.html)
Government Information Xchange
(http://www.info.gov)
Government Printing Office
(http://www.access.gpo.gov)
Government Printing Office Procurement Services
(http://www.access.gpo.gov/procurement/index.html)
GPO Access
(http://www.access.gpo.gov/su_docs/aces/aaces001.html)
GPO Gate
(http://ssdc.ucsd.edu/gpo)
Graph (EESI)
(http://www.info.usaid.gov/eesi/text/human/human2.html)
Greater Horn Information Exchange
(http://www.info.usaid.gov/HORN/index.html)
Griffiss AFB
(http://www.rl.af.mil:8001/Tour/GAFB/Griffiss.html)
Gulflink
(http://www.dtic.dla.mil/gulflink)

Hanscom AFB, MA
(http://www.hanscom.af.mil)
Harry S. Truman Library
(http://sunsite.unc.edu/lia/president/truman.html)
Harvard-Smithsonian Center for Astrophysics
(http://sao-www.harvard.edu/cfa-home.html)
Headquarters U.S. Air Force
(http://www.hq.af.mil)
Health Care Financing Administration
(http://www.hcfa.gov)
Health Services/Technology Assessment Text
(http://text.nlm.nih.gov)
Herbert Hoover Library
(http://sunsite.unc.edu/lia/president/hoover.html)
Here Today, Here Tomorrow: Varieties of Medical Ephemera
(http://www.nlm.nih.gov/exhibition/ephemera/ephemara.html)
Highly Recommended (EPA)
(http://www.epa.gov/epahome/highly.html)
Hirshhorn Museum and Sculpture Garden
(http://www.si.edu/organiza/museums/hirsh/start.htm)
Historical Archive (JFK Space Center)
(http://www.ksc.nasa.gov/history/history.html)
History of Computing (Army Research Lab)
(http://ftp.arl.mil/~mike/comphist)

History of the Internet
    (http://w3.aces.uiuc.edu/aim/scale/nethistory.html)
HIV/AIDS Prevention
    (http://www.cdc.gov/nchstp/hiv_aids/dhap.htm)
HIV Sequence Database
    (http://hiv-web.lanl.gov)
Holloman AFB
    (http://www.holloman.af.mil)
House of Representatives, The
    (http://www.house.gov)
Howard AFB
    (http://www.howard.af.mil)
HPCC K–12 Activities at Lewis Research Center
    (http://www.lerc.nasa.gov/Other_Groups/K-12/K-12_homepage.html)
HQ Air Force Personnel Center
    (http://www.afpc.af.mil)
Hubble Space Telescope (HST)
    (http://stsci.edu/EPA/Pictures.html)
Hubble Space Telescope Animations
    (http://www.stsci.edu/pubinfo/Anim.html)
Hyakutake (Comet Observation)
    (http://www.jpl.nasa.gov/comet/hyakutake)

ILIAD Library Project, The
    (http://www.jsc.nasa.gov/stb/ILIAD/Mosaic/iliad.html)
Imaging Radar
    (http://southport.jpl.nasa.gov)
Imaging Radar map
    (http://southport.jpl.nasa.gov/imagemaps)
Information about Records Retained by Presidential Libraries
    (http://clio.nara.gov:70/inform/library)
Information and Technology (ERIC)
    (gopher://ericir.syr.edu:70/11/Clearinghouses/16houses/CIT)
Infoseek
    (http://www.infoseek.com)
Innovation Network, The (NMAH)
    (http://innovate.si.edu)
Inside Information
    (UncleSam@cais.com)
Interactive Citizens Handbook
    (http://www.whitehouse.gov/WH/html/handbook.html)
Interactive Weather Information Network
    (http://iwin.nws.noaa.gov/iwin/main.html)
Internal Revenue Service
    (http://www.irs.ustreas.gov)
International Cancer Information Center
    (http://wwwicic.nci.nih.gov)
International Comet Quarterly
    (http://sao-www.harvard.edu/cfa/ps/icq.html)
International Space Station
    (http://leonardo.jsc.nasa.gov:80/ss)
International Trade Administration
    (http://www.ita.doc.gov)
Internet Grateful Med
    (http://igm.nlm.nih.gov)
Internet Law Library
    (http://law.house.gov)
Internet Resources for Student Advising
    (http://www.usia.gov/education/advise.html)

JASON Project
    (http://seawifs.gsfc.nasa.gov/scripts/JASON.html)
Jet Propulsion Laboratory
    (http://www.jpl.nasa.gov)
Jet Propulsion Laboratory Radar Imaging
    (http://southport.jpl.nasa.gov/video.html)
Jimmy Carter Library
    (http://sunsite.unc.edu/lia/president/carter.html)
John C. Stennis Space Center
    (http://www.ssc.nasa.gov)
John F. Kennedy Center for the Performing Arts ArtsEdge
    (http://artsedge.kennedy-center.org)
John F. Kennedy Space Center
    (http://www.ksc.nasa.gov)
John Fitzgerald Kennedy Library
    (http://sunsite.unc.edu/lia/president/kennedy.html)
Johnson Space Center
    (http://www.jsc.nasa.gov)
JSC Digital Images Collection
    (http://images.jsc.nasa.gov)
Just for Fun! (NASA)
    (http://www.gsfc.nasa.gov/education/just_for_fun/fun_home.html)
Justice Information Center
    (http://www.ncjrs.org)

Kadena AB, Okinawa
    (http://www.kadena.af.mil)
Keesler AFB, MS
    (http://www.kee.aetc.af.mil)
Kelly AFB, TX
    (http://www.kelly-afb.org)
Korean War Project, The
    (http://www.onramp.net/~hbarker/
Kunsan AB, Korea
    (http://www.kunsan.af.mil)

Lackland AFB, TX
    (http://www.lak.aetc.af.mil)
Lajes AFB
    (http://www.lajes.af.mil)
Langley AFB
    (http://www.langley.af.mil)
Langley Research Center
    (http://www.larc.nasa.gov)
Languages and Linguistics (ERIC)
    (http://ericir.syr.edu/ericll)
Large Scale Phenomenon Network of the International Halley Watch
    (http://eyes.gsfc.nasa.gov)
Latest Statistical Briefs on Social and Demographic Topics
    (http://www.census.gov/socdemo/www)
Laughlin AFB, TX
    (http://www.lau.aetc.af.mil)
Lawrence Livermore National Laboratory
    (http://www.llnl.gov)
LC MARVEL (Library of Congress)
    (gopher://marvel.loc.gov)
Learning About the Holocaust
    (http://www.ushmm.org/holo.htm)
Learning Web, The (USGS)
    (http://www.usgs.gov/education/index.html)

Marine and Coastal Geology Program
  (http://marine.usgs.gov)
Marines
  (http://www.usmc.mil/marines/default.htm)
Marital Status and Living Arrangements
  (http://www.census.gov/population/www/ms-la.html)
Market Place (Census Bureau)
  (http://www.census.gov/mp/www/index2.html)
Marketplace (HUD)
  (http://www.hud.gov/business.html)
Mars Exploration
  (http://www.jpl.nasa.gov/mars)
Mars Global Surveyor
  (http://mgs-www.jpl.nasa.gov)
Mars Pathfinder
  (http://mpfwww.jpl.nasa.gov)
Maxwell AFB, AL
  (http://www.aetc.af.mil/AETC-Bases/maxwell.html)
Member Information (House of Representatives)
  (http://www.house.gov/Orgpubs.html)
Microworlds
  (http://www.lbl.gov/MicroWorlds)
Minority Business Development Agency
  (http://www.doc.gov/agencies/mbda/index.html)
Minot AFB
  (http://www.minot.af.mil)
Mission to Planet Earth
  (http://www.hq.nasa.gov/office/mtpe)
Moody AFB, GA
  (http://www.moody.af.mil)
Morbidity and Mortality Weekly Report
  (http://www.cdc.gov/epo/mmwr/mmwr.html)
Motion Picture and Television Reading Room
  (http://lcweb.loc.gov/rr/mopic)
Mountain Home AFB, ID
  (http://www.mountainhome.af.mil)

Name Frequency Database
  (http://www.census.gov/genealogy/www/freqnames.html)
NARA Government Information Locator Service
  (http://www.nara.gov/gils/gils.html)
NARA Office of the Federal Register
  (http://www.access.gpo.gov/nara/index.html)
NASA Headquarters
  (http://www.hq.nasa.gov)
NASA Internet Educational Resources
  (http://quest.arc.nasa.gov/OER/EDRC22.html)
NASA Procurement Homepage
  (http://procure.msfc.nasa.gov/nasaproc.html)
NASA Programs for Individuals
  (http://university.gsfc.nasa.gov/individual.html)
NASA Public Affairs
  (http://www.nasa.gov/hqpao/hqpao_home.html)
NASA Scientific and Technical Information Program
  (http://www.sti.nasa.gov/STI-homepage.html)
NASA Spacelink
  (http://spacelink.msfc.nasa.gov)
NASA Technical Reports Service
  (http://techreports.larc.nasa.gov/cgi-bin/NTRS)
NASA Video Catalog
  (http://www.sti.nasa.gov/videocat/_COVER.htm)

NASA Video Gallery
   (http://www.hq.nasa.gov/office/pao/Library/video)
National Academy Press
   (http://www.ota.nap.edu)
National Academy of Sciences
   (http://www.nas.edu)
National Aeronautics and Space Administration
   (http://www.nasa.gov)
National Agricultural Statistics Service
   (http://www.usda.gov/nass)
National Agriculture Library
   (http://www.nalusda.gov)
National AIDS Clearinghouse
   (http://www.cdcnac.org)
National Air and Space Museum
   (http://www.nasm.edu)
National Archives Fax-On-Demand System
   (http://gopher.nara.gov:70/0/about/faxdem.txt)
National Archives and Records Administration
   (http://www.nara.gov)
National Biological Service
   (http://www.nbs.gov)
National Cancer Institute
   (http://www.nci.nih.gov)
National Center on Adult Literacy
   (http://litserver.literacy.upenn.edu)
National Center for Atmospheric Research
   (http://www.ucar.edu)
National Center for Biotechnology Information
   (http://www.ncbi.nlm.nih.gov)
National Center for Chronic Disease Prevention
   (http://www.cdc.gov/nccdphp/nccdhome.htm)
National Center for Education Statistics
   (http://www.ed.gov/NCES)
National Center for Environmental Health
   (http://www.cdc.gov/nceh/i:/cehweb/nceh/Oncehhom.htm)
National Center for Health Statistics
   (http://www.cdc.gov/nchswww/nchshome.htm)
National Center for HIV, Sexually Transmitted Diseases, and Tuberculosis
   (http://www.cdc.gov/nchstp/od/nchstp.html)
National Center for Human Genome Research
   (http://www.nchgr.nih.gov)
National Center for Infectious Diseases
   (http://www.cdc.gov/ncidod/ncid.htm)
National Center for Research Resources
   (http://www.ncrr.nih.gov)
National Center for Research in Vocational Education
   (http://vocserve.berkeley.edu)
National Centers for Environmental Prediction
   (http://www.ncep.noaa.gov)
National Clearinghouse for Bilingual Education
   (http://www.ncbe.gwu.edu)
National Climatic Data Center
   (http://www.ncdc.noaa.gov)
National Criminal Justice Research Service
   (http://www.ncjrs.org)
National Defense University
   (http://www.ndu.edu)
National Early Childhood Technical Assistance System
   (http://www.nectas.unc.edu)

National Earthquake Information Center
    (http://wwwneic.cr.usgs.gov)
National Endowment for the Arts
    (http://arts.endow.gov)
National Endowment for the Humanities
    (http://www.neh.fed.us)
National Endowment for the Humanities Grants
    (http://www.neh.fed.us/documents/over.html)
National Energy Research Supercomputer Center
    (http://www.nersc.gov)
National Estuary Program
    (http://www.epa.gov/nep/nep.html)
National Eye Institute
    (http://www.nei.nih.gov)
National Flood Insurance Program
    (http://www.fema.gov/fema/finifp.html)
National Gallery of Art, The
    (http://www.si.edu/organiza/affil/natgal/start.htm)
National Geospacial Data Clearinghouse
    (http://edcwww.cr.usgs.gov/nsdi/digital2.htm)
National Health Information Center, The
    (http://nhic-nt.health.org)
National Heart, Lung and Blood Institute
    (http://www.nhlbi.nih.gov/nhlbi/nhlbi.html)
National Highway Transportation Safety Administration, The
    (http://www.nhtsa.dot.gov)
National Hurricane Center
    (http://www.nhc.noaa.gov)
National Information Infrastructure
    (http://nii.nist.gov)
National Institute on Alcohol Abuse and Alcoholism
    (http://www.niaaa.nih.gov)
National Institute of Allergy and Infectious Diseases
    (gopher://gopher.niaid.nih.gov:70/11/aids)
    (http://www.niaid.nih.gov)
National Institute of Arthritis and Musculoskeletal and Skin Diseases
    (http://www.nih.gov/niams)
National Institute of Child Health and Human Development
    (http://www.nih.gov/nichd)
National Institute of Dental Research
    (http://www.nidr.nih.gov)
National Institute of Diabetes and Digestive and Kidney Diseases
    (http://www.niddk.nih.gov)
National Institute on Drug Abuse
    (http://www.nida.nih.gov)
National Institute of General Medical Sciences
    (http://www.nih.gov/nigms)
National Institute for Literacy
    (http://novel.nifl.gov)
National Institute of Mental Health
    (http://www.nimh.nih.gov)
National Institute of Neurological Disorders and Stroke
    (http://www.nih.gov/ninds)
National Institute of Nursing Research
    (http://www.nih.gov/ninr)
National Institute for Occupational Safety and Health
    (http://www.cdc.gov/niosh/homepage.html)
National Institute of Standards of Technology
    (http://www.nist.gov)
National Institutes of Health
    (http://www.nih.gov/home.html)

National Landslide Information Center
(http://gldage.cr.usgs.gov/html_files/nlicsun.html)
National Library of Australia
(http://www.nla.gov.au)
National Library of Canada
(http://www.nlc-bnc.ca)
National Library of The Czech Republic, Prague
(http://alpha.nkp.cz/welcome_eng.html)
National Library of Education, The
(http://www.ed.gov/NLE)
National Library of Estonia
(http://mercury.nlib.ee/index.html)
National Library of France
(http://web.culture.fr/culture/sedocum/bnf.htm)
National Library of Malaysia
(http://www.pnm.my)
National Library of Medicine, The
(http://www.nlm.nih.gov)
National Library Service for the Blind and Physically Handicapped
(http://lcweb.loc.gov/nls/nls.html)
National Library of Spain
(http://www.bne.es)
National Mapping Information
(http://www-nmd.usgs.gov)
National Marine Fisheries Service
(http://kingfish.ssp.nmfs.gov)
National Museum of African Art
(http://www.si.edu/organiza/museums/africart/start.htm)
National Museum of American Art
(http://www.si.edu/organiza/museums/amerart/start.htm)
National Museum of American History
(http://www.si.edu/organiza/museums/nmah/start.htm)
National Museum of the American Indian
(http://www.si.edu/organiza/museums/amerind/start.htm)
National Museum of Natural History
(http://www.si.edu/organiza/museums/nmnh/start.htm)
National Network of Libraries of Medicine
(http://www.nnlm.nlm.nih.gov)
National Network of Regional Educational Laboratories
(http://www.nwrel.org/national/regional-labs.html)
National Oceanic and Atmospheric Administration
(http://www.noaa.gov)
National Optical Astronomy Observatories
(http://www.noao.edu/noao.html)
National Parent Information Network (ERIC)
(http://ericps.ed.uiuc.edu/npin/npinhome.html)
National Park Service
(http://www.nps.gov)
National Performance Review
(http://www.npr.gov)
National Portrait Gallery
(http://www.si.edu/organiza/museums/portgal/start.htm)
National Postal Museum
(http://www.si.edu/organiza/museums/postal/start.htm)
National Radio Astronomy Observatory
(http://info.aoc.nrao.edu)
National Railroad Passenger Corporation
(http://www.amtrak.com)
National Register of Historic Places
(http://www.cr.nps.gov/nr/home.html)

National Rehabilitation Information Center, The
    (http://www.naric.com/naric/home.html)
National Renewable Energy Laboratory
    (http://info.nrel.gov)
National Research Center on Student Learning
    (http://www.lrdc.pitt.edu)
National Science Foundation
    (http://stis.nsf.gov)
    (http://www.nsf.gov)
National Science Foundation Grants
    (http://www.nsf.gov/nsf/homepage/grants.htm)
National Security Agency
    (http://www.nsa.gov:8080)
National Space Science Data Center
    (http://nssdc.gsfc.nasa.gov)
National Space Science Data Center Photo Gallery
    (http://nssdc.gsfc.nasa.gov/photo_gallery)
National Technical Information Service, The
    (http://www.fedworld.gov/ntis/ntishome.html)
National Technology Transfer Center
    (http://www.nttc.edu)
National Technology Transfer Center's U.S. Government Information Sources Webpage
    (http://iridium.nttc.edu/gov_res.html)
National Transportation Library, The
    (http://www.bts.gov/smart/smart.html)
National Weather Service
    (http://www.nws.noaa.gov)
National Weather Service, Central Region
    (http://www.crhnwscr.noaa.gov)
National Weather Service, Eastern Region
    (http://www.nws.noaa.gov/eastern.HTM)
National Weather Service, Pacific Region
    (http://www.nws.noaa.gov/pr/pacific.HTM)
National Weather Service, Southern Region
    (http://www.nws.noaa.gov/southern.HTM)
National Weather Service, Western Region
    (http://ssd.wrh.noaa.gov/index.html)
National Weather Service's Interactive Weather Information Network (IWIN)
    (http://iwin.nws.noaa.gov/iwin/graphicsversion/main.html)
National Weather Service Weather Videos
    (http://iwin.nws.noaa.gov/iwin/videos/videos.html)
National Wetlands Inventory
    (http://www.nwi.fws.gov)
National Wildlife Refuge System, The
    (http://bluegoose.arw.r9.fws.gov)
National Zoo Cinema
    (http://www.si.edu/organiza/muscums/zoo/homepage/hilights/cinema.htm)
National Zoological Park
    (http://www.si.edu/organiza/museums/zoo/start.htm)
Natural Resources Conservation Service
    (http://www.ncg.nrcs.usda.gov)
Naval Medical Research Institute
    (http://www.matmo.army.mil/home.html)
Naval Observatory
    (http://www.usno.navy.mil/home.html)
Naval Observatory Master Clock, The
    (http://tycho.usno.navy.mil)
Naval Research Laboratory
    (http://www.nrl.navy.mil)
Naval Research Laboratory Library
    (http://infonext.nrl.navy.mil/job.html)

Naval Undersea Warfare Center
    (http://www.nuwc.navy.mil)
Navigating the Electronic Smithsonian
    (http://www.si.edu/electrsi/navigate.htm)
Navigation Center (USCG)
    (http://www.navcen.uscg.mil)
Navy Public Affairs Library
    (http://www.navy.mil/navpalib/.www/welcome.html)
NEH Projects
    (http://www.neh.fed.us/documents/online.html)
Nellis AFB, NV
    (http://www.nellis.af.mil)
NetCast (NOAA)
    (http://nic.noaa.gov/weather.html)
Network Information Center
    (http://nic.noaa.gov)
Newark AFB, OH
    (http://www.newark.af.mil)
New Millennium Program
    (http://nmp.jpl.nasa.gov)
Newspaper and Current Periodical Reading Room
    (http://lcweb.loc.gov/global/ncp/ncp.html)
Ninth Circuit (U.S. Court of Appeals)
    (http://www.law.vill.edu/Fed-Ct/ca09.html)
Nixon Presidential Materials Staff
    (http://sunsite.unc.edu/lia/president/nixon.html)
NOAA System Acquisition Office
    (http://www.sao.noaa.gov/procure.html)
NOAA's National Climatic Data Center
    (http://www.ncdc.noaa.gov)
NOAA's National Geophysical Data Center
    (http://www.ngdc.noaa.gov)
NOAA's National Oceanographic Data Center
    (http://www.nodc.noaa.gov)
North American Breeding Bird Survey
    (http://www.mbr.nbs.gov/bbs/bbs.html)
Norwegian National Library
    (http://mack.nbr.no/e_index.html)
NTIS Alert
    (http://www.fedworld.gov/ntis/alerts.htm)
    (http://www.ntis.gov)
NTIS Bibliographic Database
    (http://www.fedworld.gov/ntis/ntisdb.htm)
Nuclear Regulatory Commission
    (http://www.nrc.gov)

Oak Ridge National Laboratory
    (http://www.ornl.gov)
Occupational Information Network (ONET)
    (http://www.doleta.gov/programs/onet/onet_hp.htm)
Occupational Outlook Handbook
    (http://stats.bls.gov/ocohome.htm)
Occupational Safety and Health Administration
    (http://www.osha.gov)
Ocean Planet
    (http://seawifs.gsfc.nasa.gov/ocean_planet.html)
Office of Air and Radiation (EPA)
    (http://www.epa.gov/oar/oarhome.html)
Office of the Assistant Secretary for Planning and Evaluation
    (http://aspe.os.dhhs.gov)

Office of Defense Programs
(http://www.dp.doe.gov)
Office of Educational Research and Improvement
(http://www.ed.gov/pubs/TeachersGuide/pt15.html)
Office of Elementary and Secondary Education (Smithsonian)
(http://www.si.edu/organiza/offices/elemsec/start.htm)
Office of Fellowships and Grants (Smithsonian Research Center)
(http://www.si.edu/organiza/offices/fellow/start.htm)
Office of Human Radiation Experiments
(http://www.ohre.doe.gov)
Office of Justice Programs
(http://www.ncjrs.org/ojphome.htm)
Office of Legislative Affairs (NASA)
(http://www.hq.nasa.gov/office/legaff)
Office of Life and Microgravity Sciences and Applications
(http://mercury.hq.nasa.gov/office/olmsa)
Office of Management and Budget
(http://www.whitehouse.gov/WH/EOP/OMB/html/ombhome.html)
Office of Minority Health
(http://www.os.dhhs.gov/progorg/ophs/omh)
Office of National Drug Control Policy
(http://www.whitehouse.gov/WH/EOP/ondcp/html/ondcp.html)
Office of Polar Program
(http://www.nsf.gov:80/od/opp/start.htm)
Office of Post-Secondary Education
(http://www.ed.gov/offices/OPE)
Office of Printing and Photographic Services
(http://www.si.edu/organiza/offices/photo/start.htm)
Office of Private Sector Relations
(http://www.peacecorps.gov/www/opsr/OPSR1.html)
Office of Procurement (NASA)
(http://www.hq.nasa.gov/office/procurement)
Office of Property Disposal
(http://www.gsa.gov/pbs/pr/prhome.htm)
Office of Research (USIA)
(http://www.usia.gov/usiahome/medreac.html)
Office of Research and Statistics (SSA)
(http://www.ssa.gov/statistics/ors_home.html)
Office of Science and Technology Policy
(http://www.whitehouse.gov/WH/EOP/OSTP/html/OSTP_Home.html)
Office of Science Education Programs (DOE)
(http://www.doe.gov/html/ouse/ousehome.html)
Office of Space Communications
(http://mercury.hq.nasa.gov/office/spacecom)
Office of Space Flight
(http://www.osf.hq.nasa.gov)
Office of Space Science
(http://www.hq.nasa.gov/office/oss)
Office of Strategic Phenomena
(http://vader.nrl.navy.mil/osp.html)
Office of Volunteer Recruitment and Selection
(http://www.peacecorps.gov/www/vrs/VRS1.html)
Office of Water (EPA)
(http://www.epa.gov/OW)
Official Space Shuttle Homepage
(http://shuttle.nasa.gov)
Online Exhibit Hall (NARA)
(http://www.nara.gov/exhall/exhibits.html)
On-Line Images from the History of Medicine
(http://wwwoli.nlm.nih.gov/databases/olihmd/olihmd.html)

Open Net (DOE)
  (http://www.doe.gov/html/osti/opennet/openscr.html)
Organization and Operations (House of Representatives)
  (http://www.house.gov/Orgops.html)
Osan AB, Korea
  (http://www.osan.af.mil)

Pacific Air Forces
  (http://www.hqpacaf.af.mil)
Pamphlet Rack, The (SSA)
  (http://www.ssa.gov/programs/pamphlet_rack.html)
Park Net—National Park Service
  (http://www.nps.gov)
Particle Adventure, The
  (http://pdg.lbl.gov/cpep/adventure.html)
Partnerships Against Violence
  (http://www.usdoj.gov/pavnet.html)
Patent Bibliographic Database
  (http://patents.cnidr.org:4242)
Patent and Trademark Office
  (http://www.uspto.gov)
Peace Corps
  (http://www.peacecorps.gov)
Peace Corps Chronological History
  (http://www.peacecorps.gov/www/press/Press5.html)
Pearl Harbor, HI
  (http://www.pac.disa.mil)
Pension and Welfare Benefits Administration
  (http://www.dol.gov/dol/pwba)
People (Smithsonian)
  (http://www.si.edu/people/start.htm)
Periodicals
  (http://lcweb.loc.gov/global/ncp/oltitles.html)
Persian Gulf Veterans' Illness
  (http://www.va.gov/health/environ/persgulf.htm)
Perspectives (Smithsonian)
  (http://www.si.edu/perspect/start.htm)
Photo Library, The (FEMA)
  (http://www.fema.gov/fema/photo.html)
Pioneer Project
  (http://pyroeis.arc.nasa.gov/pioneer/PNhome.html)
Planetary Exploration
  (http://www.jpl.nasa.gov/mip/planet.html)
Planetary Rings Node, The
  (http://ringside.arc.nasa.gov)
Planet Earth (DOD)
  (http://www.nosc.mil/planet_earth/info.html)
Planning a Visit (Smithsonian)
  (http://www.si.edu/welcome/planvis/start.htm)
PLANTS Database (Department of Agriculture)
  (http://plants.usda.gov:80/plants)
Pop Clocks
  (http://www.census.gov/main/www/popclock.html)
Population Division Home Page
  (http://www.census.gov/population/www)
Postage Rates
  (http://www.usps.gov/consumer/rates.htm)
Preparing for a Disaster
  (http://www.fema.gov/fema/predis.html)
Preparing Your Child for College
  (http://www.ed.gov/pubs/Prepare)

President John F. Kennedy Assassination Records Collection
    (http://www.nara.gov/nara/jfk/jfk.html)
Presidential Library System
    (http://clio.nara.gov/nara/president/address.html)
Procurement-related hotlist
    (http://www.sba.gov/hotlist)
Products (Smithsonian)
    (http://www.si.edu/products/start.htm)
Programs and Services (Education Department)
    (http://www.ed.gov/programs.html)
Project Galileo
    (http://www.jpl.nasa.gov/galileo)
Public Affairs (JFK Space Center)
    (http://www-pao.ksc.nasa.gov/kscpao/kscpao.htm)
Public Broadcasting Online Directory
    (http://www.cpb.org/directory/home.html)
Publications for Parents
    (http://www.ed.gov/pubs/parents.html)

Quest! The K–12 Internet Initiative
    (http://quest.arc.nasa.gov)

RAF Lakenheath, UK
    (http://www.usafe.af.mil/bases/laken/laken.htm)
Randolph AFB, TX
    (http://www.aetc.af.mil/AETC-Bases/randolph.html)
Reading, English and Communication (ERIC)
    (http://www.indiana.edu/~eric_rec)
Regional Offices (EPA)
    (http://www.epa.gov/epahome/Regions.html)
Regional Offices (NOAA)
    (http://nic.noaa.gov/regional_map.html)
Regional Offices (SBA)
    (http://www.sbaonline.sba.gov/regions/regionmap.html)
Regional Resource and Federal Centers
    (http://www.aed.org/special.ed/rrfc1.html)
Reinventing Schools
    (http://www.nap.edu/nap/online/techgap/welcome.html)
Renwick Gallery
    (http://www.si.edu/organiza/museums/renwick/start.htm)
Representatives' e-mail addresses
    (http://www.house.gov/Whoswho.html)
Research and Development Division (NHTSA)
    (http://www.nhtsa.dot.gov/nrd/index.html)
Resources for Greek and Latin Classics
    (http://lcweb.loc.gov/global/classics/classics.html)
Reusable Launch Vehicle Quick Time Movies
    (http://rlv.msfc.nasa.gov/rlv_htmls/RLVMovies.html)
Reusable Launch Vehicle Technology Program
    (http://rlv.msfc.nasa.gov)
Robins AFB, GA
    (http://www.robins.af.mil)
Ronald Reagan Library
    (http://sunsite.unc.edu/lia/president/reagan.html)
Royal Library, The, Denmark
    (http://www.kb.bib.dk)
Rural Education and Small Schools (ERIC)
    (http://www.ael.org/~eric/eric.html)

SAREX—Shuttle Amateur Radio Experiment
    (http://www.gsfc.nasa.gov/sarex/sarex_mainpage.html)

Tennessee Valley Authority
    (http://www.tva.gov)
Tenth Circuit (U.S. Court of Appeals)
    (http://www.law.emory.edu/10circuit)
Thematic mapping system (Census Bureau)
    (http://www.census.gov/themapit/www)
Third Circuit (U.S. Court of Appeals)
    (http://www.law.vill.edu/Fed-Ct/ca03.html)
THOMAS
    (http://thomas.loc.gov)
TIGER Mapping Service (Census Bureau)
    (http://tiger.census.gov)
Tiger maps (Census Bureau)
    (http://tiger.census.gov/instruct.html)
Tinker AFB, OK
    (http://www1.tinker.af.mil/default.htm)
    (http://www1.tinker.af.mil)
TOPEX/POSEIDON Project, The
    (http://topex-www.jpl.nasa.gov)
Tour the Facilities (JFK Space Center)
    (http://www.ksc.nasa.gov/facilities/tour.html)
Traumatic Stress Homepage, The
    (http://www.long-beach.va.gov/ptsd/stress.html)
Travel Information (CDC)
    (http://www.cdc.gov/travel/travel.html)
Travis AFB, CA
    (http://www.travis.af.mil)
Trinity Symposium (Department of Energy)
    (http://www2.dp.doe.gov/MapServe/text/TRINITY.HTM)
Tropical Prediction Center
    (http://www.nhc.noaa.gov)
Twelve Federal Reserve Districts
    (http://www.clev.frb.org/fedlinks.htm)
Tyndall AFB, FL
    (http://admin.325lg.tyndall.af.mil/index.html)

U.S. Agency for International Development
    (http://www.info.usaid.gov)
U.S. Agency for International Development Regional Information
    (http://www.info.usaid.gov/welcome/imap/imap.html)
U.S. Air Force Academy
    (http://www.usafa.af.mil)
U.S. Air Force Acquisition Page
    (http://www.hq.af.mil/SAFAQ)
U.S. Air Force Europe
    (http://www.usafe.af.mil)
U.S. Army Acquisitions
    (http://www.sarda.army.mil)
U.S. Army Corps of Engineers Information Network
    (http://www.usace.army.mil)
U.S. Army War College
    (http://carlisle-www.army.mil)
U.S. Attorneys (DOJ)
    (http://gopher.usdoj.gov/usao/usao.html)
U.S. Budget Site
    (gopher://gopher.stat-usa.gov:70/11/BudgetFY96)
U.S. Business Advisor (White House)
    (http://www.business.gov)
U.S. Coast Guard, The
    (http://www.dot.gov/dotinfo/uscg)

USS Carl Vinson
(http://www.navy.mil/homepages/cvn70)
USS Constitution
(http://www.navy.mil/homepages/constitution)
USS Dwight D. Eisenhower
(http://www.navy.mil/homepages/cvn69)
USS Hawes
(http://www.navy.mil/homepages/uss-hawes)
USS John C. Stennis
(http://www.navy.mil/homepages/jcs)

Vance AFB, OK
(http://www.vnc.aetc.af.mil)
VA Online: The VA Bulletin Board
(telnet://vaonline.va.gov)
Veterans Affairs BBS, VA Online
(telnet://vaonline.va.gov)
Veterans Benefits Manual
(http://www.va.gov/publ/benman96)
Vietnam Era POW/MIA Database
(http://lcweb2.loc.gov/pow/powhome.html)
Views of the Solar System
(http://bang.lanl.gov/solarsys)
Views of the Solar System Images and Animations
(http://bang.lanl.gov/solarsys/raw/index.htm)
Villanova's Federal Web Locator
(http://www.law.vill.edu/Fed-Agency/fedwebloc.html)
Virtual Tour of the Capitol
(http://www.senate.gov/capitol/virtour.html)
Visible Human Project, The
(http://www.nlm.nih.gov/research/visible/visible_human.html)
Visiting the U.S. Senate
(http://www.senate.gov/tour/tour.html)
Visitor Information (House of Representatives)
(http://www.house.gov/Visitor.html)
Visit Your National Parks
(http://www.nps.gov/parks.html)
Voice of America
(http://www.voa.gov)
Voyager Project
(http://vraptor.jpl.nasa.gov/voyager/voyager.html)

Wallops Flight Facility
(http://www.wff.nasa.gov)
Walter Reed Army Institute of Research
(http://www.wramc.amedd.army.mil)
Water Resources of the United States
(http://h2o.usgs.gov)
Web Interactive Network of Government Services
(http://www.wings.usps.gov/index.html)
Welcome to the Planets!
(http://stardust.jpl.nasa.gov/planets)
Whale Songs
(http://kingfish.ssp.nmfs.gov:80/songs.html)
What Every Investor Should Know
(http://www.sec.gov/invkhome.htm)
Where to Write for Vital Records
(http:// www.cdc.gov/nchswww/w2w-all.htm)
White House, The
(http://www.whitehouse.gov)

Index

WE WANT TO HEAR FROM YOU!

As you navigate Uncle Sam's domain, we're sure you will come across websites that merit inclusion in the next edition of *The Great American Web Book*. Or, you may find that a site we included has changed its address. Let us know! We encourage your comments, suggestions, and corrections. Please e-mail us at:

UncleSam@cais.com

And please visit our new website, where you'll find links to many of the sites described in this book. We'll be updating our homepage often to highlight new treasures, reports, websites, changed addresses, and more. Our URL is:

http://www.uncle-sam.com/unclesam

COMING SOON FROM *INSIDE INFORMATION*

The Great American Web Book is the first in a series of books that Inside Information is producing in order to make government information more accessible to you. Our next book will be *Uncle Sam's Guide to the Great Outdoors,* a remarkably comprehensive guide to America's outdoor treasures, from national parks and wildlife refuges to national monuments and seashores. Random House will publish this book next year.